Teaching Drama
A mind of many wonders

Norah Morgan and Juliana Saxton

Stanley Thornes (Publishers) Ltd

Originally published in 1987 by
Hutchinson Education
Reprinted 1988 (twice)

Reprinted in 1989 by
Stanley Thornes (Publishers) Ltd
Old Station Drive
Leckhampton
CHELTENHAM GL53 0DN

Reprinted 1991
Reprinted 1992

British Library Cataloguing in Publication Data

Morgan, Norah
    Teaching drama.
    1. Drama—Study and teaching
    I. Title   II. Saxton, Juliana
    792'.07'1   PN1701

ISBN 0 7487 0243 1

Printed and bound in Great Britain at
The Bath Press, Avon

Contents

This book is dedicated to Ted Morgan
and Joanna Saxton who suffered long
and were kind.

'So i say to be capible it is to have
a mind of many wounder's'

quoted in NADIE Papers no. 1,
(Australia, 1984)

Foreword

In recent years, drama in education has been given a sound basis in theory and practice by such outstanding teachers as Gavin Bolton and Dorothy Heathcote. Research and observation have confirmed the usefulness of drama strategies to teachers of many curriculum subjects and at all age levels. It has become clear that interest, motivation and learning all result when drama is employed for educational ends. One might expect that such strategies would by now be used by many teachers to enrich and illuminate the curriculum.

The reality is different. In the American Association Theatre for Youth's *Youth Theatre Journal* (Autumn 1986), in a study of a number of American elementary schools, Roger Bedard noted the absence, not just of significant drama experiences being offered to children, but the lack of drama activities of any kind. This bleak picture is also likely to be true of many British schools, in spite of lip-service paid to the notion of drama as a facilitating element in the curriculum. Some teachers use the dramatic mode as a way of communicating and understanding, and take their students towards a collective act of giving form to experience, but they are too few. Those of us engaged in the initial or in-service training of teachers in drama must ask ourselves why, in spite of courses, workshops, handbooks and resource materials, drama in education has made so little impact on the practice of the majority of teachers in our schools.

In drama, teachers and students are engaged in collective enquiry and exploration. Learning is likely to occur through co-operation, interaction and participation. Drama teachers need to have at their command a wide range of personal skills and interactive techniques, as well as a sound understanding of the nature of drama and theatre. They need the ability to structure a lesson, not just for the transmission of information but for the shaping of a shared learning experience. They need considerable powers of observation, perception and organization. They must be process-oriented. They need to be able, not just to answer students' questions, but to ask questions which lead to the formulation of more important questions by their students. At present, very few training courses provide the apprentice teacher with these skills or the means of developing what Jerome Bruner has called a 'drama-creating personality', in other words the ability to create significant learning experiences in the classroom. Good teachers, Bruner points out, are human events, not transmission devices.

Dorothy Heathcote, whose own innovative practice has been such an inspiration to teachers throughout the world, has been concerned for many years at these omissions in the training of teachers. She has always known that effective drama teaching depends on the 'minute particulars' of the teacher's skills. These skills, for Heathcote, include the ability to select, to focus, to distort productively, to 'sign' effectively, to handle language with significance, to question with implication, to promote reflection – all of them central concerns in this book.

Morgan and Saxton are committed to the belief that it is possible to train teachers in the kind of thinking and planning which leads to successful drama teaching. But they are realistic. They know teachers and schools. They understand that drama teaching can make enormous demands on personal confidence and security, and that teachers are always concerned at some level with problems of control and predictability. Loss of physical control of the lesson may be less worrying to the teacher than the loss of control of the ideas which are developed. Morgan and Saxton have analyzed many of the ways in which teachers can continue to shape the ideas and activities of the lesson from within the work, and the strategies through which the teacher's capacity to transfer power and autonomy to students is strengthened, not weakened. They appreciate the problems, anxieties and insecurities which face teachers trying to work in this kind of 'open possibility', but their book goes far beyond the 'safety-net' which they modestly aim to provide. They succeed in clarifying and categorizing the key understandings and techniques which will lead to fruitful learning encounters in drama.

Morgan and Saxton have built their theories on precise observation and sound practice. They share with us their knowledge, not just of *what* to do in the drama lesson, but of *how* to do it. The intellectual strength, good humour and sound common sense which underly their practice are also at the heart of this book. It will give teachers the courage and capacity to discover for themselves and their students the power of drama as a medium for learning.

Cecily O'Neill
May, 1987

Introduction

This book is not only for those teachers who use drama to promote understanding of many subject areas at the primary, elementary and secondary level. It is also for those teachers who work towards performance and who believe that knowledge and practice in the art form of theatre challenge and extend human experience.

The learning environment in a drama or theatre class makes demands on both teacher and students which are different from those in a classroom environment, where knowledge and skills are pre-eminent. Knowledge and skills are important in drama, but learning comes through the negotiation of this knowledge and these skills. Both students and teacher are operating in an imagined or fictitious situation where there is no one right solution, only the appropriate one. Therefore, the planning and conducting of such lessons require special attention.

When teaching drama or theatre, it is not enough for the teacher to know *what* to do. It is important for the teacher to know *why* she is doing what she is doing and *how* to do it, because every class and student is different.

We hope this book will provide a safety net for the inexperienced teacher, new frames of reference for experienced teachers and some useful 'whats' for all teachers.

For ease of reading and in the interests of sexual equality, we have chosen to refer to the teacher as 'she' and the student as 'he'.

We have used many examples from our own teaching experience. These examples might give the impression that all our students are disciplined, intelligent and sensitive, that our classes are models of structuring and that our teaching is always dynamic and witty! Let us assure you that we have had our share of pedestrian work, but it would not do to bore you with that!

Many of the examples are drawn from the work of teachers

and teachers-in-training at our respective universities, to whom we are deeply indebted for their enthusiasm, courage to experiment, and willingness to analyse their results and share their successes and failures with us.

We are especially grateful to the following colleagues: Helen Dunlop of the Ontario Ministry of Education for her initial encouragement; Len Popp of Brock Faculty of Education for his assistance with our taxonomies; Clive Barker for his theatrical insight; Linda Laidlaw, whose research made Chapter 5 so much easier; Bev Haskins and Grace Smith for their classroom teaching; David Booth for his demonstration lessons; and Gavin Bolton for his incisive mind and supportive criticism.

Above all, we thank Margaret Burke, who challenged, tested and never wavered in her belief in the value of this book for drama teachers and Cecily O'Neill, a brilliant teacher and writer, whose advocacy made us believe in ourselves.

Victoria, B.C.
St Catharines, Ontario
1986

1

The relationship between theatre and drama

This is a book about classroom drama, so we are going to start by talking about theatre. This is not because we want to 'get it out of the way'. It is because we have come to recognize, through observation and analysis, that the teacher who, instinctively or deliberately, makes use of the devices of the art form (theatre elements and play structure) has a better chance of achieving her educational objectives.

The drama teacher is the one who knows how to use the theatre in the service of the students' own dramatic activity and how to use drama for those who are ready to be involved in theatre presentation. Teachers of Theatre Arts at the senior levels often make little use of the explorative strategies of drama work to help students find the inner understanding necessary for the expressive action of the script, while the classroom drama teacher makes little, if any, use of the art form to help her students find the appropriate expressive frames for the meaning they are exploring. Drama and theatre are not mutually exclusive. If drama is about meaning, it is the art form of theatre which encompasses and contains that meaning. If theatre is about expression, then it is the dramatic exploration of the meaning which fuels that expression.

The elements of theatre craft

'The difference between theatre (performance) and classroom drama is that in theatre everything is contrived so that the audience gets the kicks. In the classroom the participants get the kicks. However, the roots are the same: the elements of theatre craft.'[1]

Dorothy Heathcote identifies these elements as:

Focus – a particular moment in time that captures the essence of a broad, general human experience and shows its implications.

Tension – the pressure for response that is at the heart of a dramatic action. Heathcote subdivides this into surprise; not knowing (the longer you wait to find out, the more tension you feel); complications; limitations of space and time; blocking of a plan, desire or idea.

The spectra – darkness/light; sound/silence; movement/stillness.

> In every classroom drama (Heathcote) employs the tools
> of the theatre: trapping a group into a particular
> moment, developing tension and exploiting the three
> spectra.[2]

Gavin Bolton, in *Towards a Theory of Drama in Education*, classifies the elements of theatre form as:

Tension – a sense of time; focus; surprise.

Contrast – sound/silence; movement/stillness; change of direction (from the comfortable to the uncomfortable, from threat to relief).

Symbolization – action or object or both (which must) depend on concreteness and on its power to stir deep feelings . . . (it) is something which holds many levels of meaning simultaneously.[3]

We prefer to categorize these elements in a slightly different way, while at the same time trying not to re-invent the wheel!

Focus

In a play a director has two foci: 'What is this play about?' and 'How will each scene be shaped so that it is possible for the audience to understand the overall meaning of this particular interpretation?'

In classroom drama there are also two foci: the educational focus or teaching objectives (what is to be taught) and the dramatic focus – that part of each lesson which must be framed so that the students will have opportunities to achieve a measure of understanding of the educational focus. For example, in a history lesson, the teacher has decided that her educational focus will be to examine the concept of injustice. She chooses as her dramatic context the lives of servants in 'the big house'. Her particular focus for entering the theme is the hiring line at the local fair. In order to build in the need for employment, her first activity might focus on creating the kinds of families in which parents would be prepared to indenture their children.[4] Focus always answers the question, 'Why am I asking my students to do this?' and is the key to successful teaching.

Tension

The *Oxford English Dictionary* defines tension as 'mental excitement' and we prefer this definition because it acknowledges the positive as well as the negative implications of the word. Mental excitement 'is fundamental to intellectual and emotional engagement' not only as a stimulus but as 'the bonding agent that sustains involvement in the dramatic task'.[5]

In a drama class, tension is put in by the teacher through her instructions outside the drama and/or through her role inside the drama. Tension may be injected through:

1 Challenge
   outside   'This is difficult work. I may be expecting too much.'
   inside   'But he's a Commandant! What makes you think he
           would listen to us?'

2 Limiting time
   outside   'We have a lot to get through, so I can only give you
           three minutes.'
   inside   'The guards change at midnight, so we must all be
           in place by then.'

3 Limiting space·
   outside   'All come close to me.'
   inside   'Please watch your heads, the entrance to the cave is
           very low.'

4 Constraints
   outside   'When you do this scene, you must find a way of
           conveying the feeling without touching.'
   inside   'There will be no physical contact between prisoner
           and visitor.'

5 The unknown
   outside   'I'm not quite sure what's going to happen.'
   inside   'What will he expect from us?'

6 Responsibility
   outside   'Is there anyone here who has enough knowledge to
           handle this role?'

inside   'Who will act as lookout? Our lives depend on your
            eyes and ears.'

7 Evaluation
   outside 'Let's watch this to see how well they have solved
             the problems.'
   inside   'If any one of you does not honour his oath, this
             mission will fail.'

Contrast

We, like Bolton, subsume the spectra under Contrast, but they
could equally be examined under Tension, Symbolization or
Focus.

1 Darkness/Light
   Many teachers say, 'We cannot darken the room, so we can't
   use that one.' What about 'Close your eyes?' In a fully lighted
   room, if you believe in the light of the candle, it makes the
   rest of the room dark.

   Other kinds of light and dark are: a light voice/a dark voice;
   a light moment in a tragic situation; a moment of realization
   (usually signalled in the comic papers by a light bulb going
   on!).

2 Sound/Silence
   The shout and the whisper; conversation and a pause; a flood
   of ideas *versus* silent consideration; the silence and the drip;
   the key in the lock; the ticking of the clock; the moment of
   expectation and release (the silent women waiting at the mine
   head for their sons and husbands to appear).

3 Movement/Stillness
   Resting after exertion; action after discussion; fast motion/
   slow motion; the power of depiction *versus* the power of
   improvisation; one person moving while others are still
   (Florence Nightingale at Scutari Hospital); one person still
   while everyone else is moving (the one who is left behind).

4 Peripeteia
   (a) the unexpected: Finding a chewing gum wrapper on the
   moon; finding that authority has clay feet; finding that primitive people need us less than we need them. (The first is a
   shocker, but the others require preparation for the moment
   of realization.)

(b) the unpredictable: The teacher will recognize the rich dramatic potential in what we call the unpredictable: that an enemy is a potential friend; that a villain becomes more villainous by being seen to be kind; is the bully the coward, or the coward the bully? Understanding this provides a dimension which can deepen and enrich drama work.[6]

Symbolization

The way in which the teacher draws attention to the symbol (gesture, word, object, etc.) generates a collective meaning and also gives time and opportunity for the participant to endow that symbol with his individual meaning. For example:

> The empty bowl placed in the centre of the circle signifies the hunger of the tribe. And for one it represents suffering for her children; for another it represents his failure as a provider; for another it represents the anger of the Gods . . .

Focus, Tension, Contrast and Symbolization are fundamental to generating, motivating, sustaining and crystallizing the shared, significant experience – the means by which the teacher achieves her objectives. Of equal value in the planning of a lesson or series of lessons is the framework provided by the structure of the 'well-made play'. 'That kind of play . . . which keeps to the rules designed to capture, sustain and satisfy interest.'[7] Every teacher planning a lesson is surely working with Styan's definition in mind, and a drama teacher is almost always working as a play-wright, because it is the process and not the product with which she is concerned.

The four stages of the well-made play

We are not using the term 'well-made' in the 19th century sense of a play in which the dilemmas are solved. In drama a neat resolution is often neither true nor appropriate. We mean 'well-made' in the sense of 'well-constructed'.

Exposition

This is the part of the play, usually at the beginning, which tells the audience what has happened previously.

In drama, exposition consists of the teacher and the class sharing what they already know through discussion or demonstration; agreeing on the 'rules of the game' (time, place, behaviour); clarifying understanding (word meanings and connotations); working in dramatic exercise; practising certain skills and/or exploring the context through dramatic play. In Dorothy Heathcote's words, the exposition is about letting the students know 'what's up'. It is in this part of the lesson that the teacher either finds or confirms her dramatic focus. This focus is particularized in action which is the first step of the rising action or complication.

Rising action/complication

This is the part of the play where the protagonists and the problem are introduced: situations are introduced which reveal those things that need to be understood in order to grasp the significance of the climax.

In this part of the teaching structure, the teacher is concerned with building volume (not plot); looking at the problem from many different perspectives; working forward and backward in time; using a number of strategies and techniques in the service of the students' ideas. There may be times when everyone needs to return to exposition for research or clarification. The teacher is working three-dimensionally, manipulating her teaching objectives ('the play for the teacher'), the expectations of the students ('the play for them') and the ideas that lie within the material ('the play').

Climax/Crisis

This is the part of the play where the action increases tension to a crisis.

In the complication the teacher is working without a net. She cannot plan for the climax or crisis, all she can do is look for that moment or situation which will have a collective significance, full of feeling, which is both real for the participants and appropriate to the context of the drama.

Denouement

This is the part of the play where the plot is resolved.

In drama, it is important that the participants have an opportunity to bring understanding to the feeling engendered by that significant moment. There should be, as Dorothy Heathcote points out, an opportunity for 'anagnorisis', the moment of recognition when the intelligence comes into play and provides the opening for aesthetic experiencing. The way in which the teacher handles this part of the lesson is an indication of the sensitivity of her teaching. Whether she chooses writing, discussion, narration, speaking thoughts or silent reflection, will depend upon how she feels her educational objectives can best be satisfied as a result of the dramatic experience which she and her students have undergone. The final feeling must be that of satisfaction, both for the students and the teacher, just as is the case in a successful theatre experience.

Three lesson examples

A drama lesson follows the same development as the well-made play. The material of a drama lesson, as of a play, is 'a real man in a mess'. But just as plays fail if they lack the theatrical elements and a relevance for the audience, so a drama lesson can fail for exactly the same reasons.

Below are three examples of lessons in which we have analyzed the use of theatre elements and structure. Lesson 1 was taught by Gavin Bolton, working with a class of twenty students (16–17 years old). Lesson 2 was with a class of students 12–13 years old. Lesson 3 was with a class of elementary students (10–11 years old).

Lesson 1

Educational context: Improvisation
Educational focus: In-depth drama
Dramatic context: To discover the effect of a crisis on a family
Dramatic focus: The parents
Source: 'Parents and teenaged children are in a hospital waiting for news of the condition of the oldest child who has been in a serious traffic accident.' (B.C. Drama Curriculum Guide)

Framework: Exposition	Theatre element
1 Gavin reads the extract and says, 'What we are not going to do is rely on phony, clichéd preconceptions. We use truth in drama, the truth of our own experience. I am going to ask you to explore this personally. It will be about an actual event from within your own experience.'	Tension: challenge
2 In pairs: 'Decide on a major accident which has happened to you. Exchange stories. Keep this private.'	
3 'The listener is to retell the story, as if it had happened to him, keeping the feeling quality of the original. The listener will tell how close the teller is to the original story.'	Tension: evaluation (Teller inside, listener outside)
4 In a large circle: Volunteers repeat their story to the group, with the permission of the owner of the story.	
5 After one particularly moving story: 'What is happening when you hear a story like that?' To the storyteller: 'Can you stand being further exposed?' To the group: 'Pull your chairs closer to give her more security.' To the storyteller: 'Can you repeat the end of the story?'	Tension: (a) challenge (b) the unknown
6 Students question the storyteller about the accident.	Tension: evaluation (Teller is in the 'as if'.)
7 Another story about a boy drowned at a community picnic.	
8 'Can anyone tell a story which has a lighter tone?' (Lots of laughter at this story.)	Contrast: heavy to light

Framework: Rising action	
9 Back to the source: Gavin sets two chairs inside the semicircle of students. 'I am going to begin the	Tension: (a) the unknown (b) challenge

Framework: Rising action (cont.)
improvisation, but you are not going
to act the part; you are going to
represent the parents, Mr and Mrs
Johnson, in thought.'

Theatre element
(c) responsibility

Framework: Return to exposition
'What is the sex of the injured
child?' (a boy)
A student asks, 'Are they really a
close family?'
Gavin replies, 'That is something you
will decide.'

Framework: Return to rising action

10 Gavin in role as the doctor at the
hospital. He talks to the empty
chairs. He tells them that the boy is
still unconscious: brain damage is
suspected. He wishes the parents to
sign a form for further surgery.
Without surgery the boy will regress
to vegetable status.
The students start to question the
doctor. Gavin keeps his eyes on the
empty chairs.
A student: 'How long do we have
to decide?'
'Twelve hours.'

Tension:
(a) responsibility to
    keep in role
(b) limiting time

Symbol: chairs
(Collective: These
chairs are our parents.
Individual: My
parents only work
together in a crisis.
I'm glad my parents
have the support of
each other. In my
family it would be my
mother on her own.)

Framework: Exposition

11 Questioning out of role: 'Do you
want a waiting experience or do you
want the boy to become a cabbage?
Or does he die? Or will there be a
restoration to normality, realizing
that 'normal' might be different
from pre-accident?'

Tension:
responsibility
(We cannot change
what we decide.)

12 'What exactly was the accident?'
He offers many choices from the
first stories.
The students choose a car accident as
being the most likely. The students

Framework: Exposition (cont.)	Theatre element
vote on the four choices: 4 for waiting, 6 for regression, 4 for death and none for normality.	

13 Change of space to informal group, lying on the floor. They choose a name for the victim, 'Jerry'.	Contrast: stillness to movement to stillness

Framework: Rising action

14 The students create a vocal collage of Jerry's life, speaking as any character concerned with Jerry's life. 'Feel the moment when it is right to speak. Try to develop an angle on him.' Gavin joins in with the students.	Focus moves to the boy. Tension: challenge
15 Discussion about the character they have created. (Lots of laughter) 'Did we learn anything about him?' 'Plenty! He's normal!'	Contrast: peripeteia (Tragedy: they know he isn't going to recover; comedy: he was one of us)
16 'I have an idea about the next scene we should tackle. I think it should be between Jerry and his parents. Which scene should we do?' They decide on 'buying the car'. (Students are working here as 'playwrights'.)	Contrast: the unexpected (The teacher appears uncertain!)
17 Set up family groups. Student: 'What if there is only one parent?' Gavin: 'You are pulling it away from the established rules of the drama. We already have a Mr and Mrs Johnson.' Students do the scene simultaneously (no showing). 'Is there anything you have discovered about attitudes?' He checks for the truthfulness of each situation.	Focus: boy and parents Tension: constraint (We have to obey the rules.)

Framework: Rising action (cont.)   **Theatre element**

18 Gavin separates the 'sons' from each group. 'Find a way that symbolizes "I am a person that is cut off". We are looking for the *image* of a person. Don't be satisfied with the first thing you do.'

Focus: boy
Contrast: isolation from the group; words to pictures

Each group watches their own 'son' become the brain-damaged victim.

Symbol: the action (Collective: he is no longer one of us Individual: I might have been in the car with him; does he know he's changed?)

Framework: Sub-climax

19 Pairs exercise:
'Choose a simple domestic task that Mr and Mrs Johnson would be doing together after their return from the hospital. The son isn't there but the image of him is.'

Focus: on parents
Contrast: absence of the son makes his presence more powerful.

Framework: Rising action

20 Gavin stops them after a bit.
'I am going to orchestrate snippets of these scenes. The signal to begin is when I stand beside you. When you are not "on" you will freeze.'

Tension: evaluation

21 Gavin narrates: 'Jerry is almost ready to come home. Jerry is dressed and in a chair. Jerry has not spoken yet. Mr and Mrs Johnson are visiting him in the hospital.'
Gavin demonstrates with one group. To Jerry: 'Are you able to cope with this, because the boy has already much regressed? I will stop you if I feel there is no truth. This is a very serious responsibility. When you do this you must do it very well indeed.'

Focus: on parents and son

Tension: challenge

Tension: evaluation

Framework: Rising action (cont.)	**Theatre element**
22 Gavin stops it when he sees that the demonstration is being done with integrity. 'Will you all continue now?' The other groups begin their improvisations.	As in 21.
23 He freezes the work. He puts his hand on the head of a parent. 'Say what you as a parent are feeling in your heart as you watch your own son.' He hears all the parents' concerns and stops the work quietly.	Focus: the family Contrast: improvisation to depiction
24 Narration: 'Time moves on and Jerry has regressed more and more. Will you now set up a family photograph as it once was before the accident?'	Contrast: from the darkness of the tragedy to the light of the past

Framework: Climax (Catharsis)

25 'Rearrange the photograph to contain Jerry as he now is. Jerry will not, of course, know why he is being prepared for the photograph.'	Contrast: light to darkness Symbol: the picture (Collective: the family has changed Individual: Why do we have to have him in the picture? I'll see that picture every time I go out in the car.)

Framework: Denouement (Anagnorosis)

26 'Please stand and tell us what effect this has had on your family since the accident happened.'	Tension: release through reflection in role
27 The students gather around Gavin and talk about what they have done. He acknowledges that they have done very difficult work and done it very well.	Focus: the teacher Tension: evaluation

Framework: Denouement (cont.)	**Theatre element**
28 'If we were working longer we would need to find a comic moment. Comedy can say important things about serious matters. It would not have done at the beginning of the session, but only to release this moment.'	Focus: the teacher Contrast: the teacher points out the power of contrast

A feeling of satisfaction was engendered because the students knew they had worked well for a demanding teacher. Although we have no way of knowing the lasting effect upon them, their classroom teacher has never forgotten it!

Lesson 2

Educational context: Role-playing
Educational focus: To discover that operating outside the law brings its own responsibility
Dramatic context: A play about a bank robbery (the students' choice)
Dramatic focus: The robber gang

Framework: Exposition	**Theatre element**
1 Teacher, in role, enters and informs the children that if they wish to become part of his gang they must be fully professional, that is, succeed in getting the money and leave no traces.	Focus: the robber gang Contrast: the unexpected (The teacher as gang leader)
2 The students are asked to demonstrate, in groups of five, their most successful robbery. Teacher in role and students in role may ask questions of the demonstrating group.	Tension: evaluation
3 Out of role, the class decides which pattern of operation should be followed. (The class chooses to rob a city bank with guns, leaving no clues.)	Tension: responsibility (They are stuck with what they choose)

Framework: Rising action	Theatre element
4 Teacher and class in role again. Teacher states that the time has come to plan their next robbery of the bank in High Street. Jobs are listed on the blackboard: ammunition, plan of the bank, approach and getaway, disguises, and a research group to look at accounts of other successful and unsuccessful robberies! The gang decides who will do what. Teacher in role becomes a resource.	Tension: (a) limiting time (b) constraints (c) evaluation
5 The sharing of information which involves the selection and training of the right people for the right jobs. How the money will be divided fairly in terms of duties: teacher in role, 'I, naturally, will take 40%!'	Contrast: the unexpected (We take the risks and he gets most of the money!)
6 Meeting on the afternoon before the robbery. Teacher in role sums up all that has been done: 'We are well-prepared, but no matter how often we rehearse, it will only happen once. You have all made arrangements for your families during the lying-low time, which may be for many months. You are prepared, if necessary, to kill.'	Tension: (a) limiting time (b) responsibility Contrast: the unexpected (Teacher instigating violence)
7 Teacher in role: 'Let each one now write a letter to his family, which will, I promise you, be delivered in the event that something unforeseen should occur.'	Contrast: the unpredictable (Confidence to doubt) Symbol: the letter (Collective: if this letter is ever read, I will be dead. Individual: I hope they know I did it for them; they'll be glad I'm dead; this is one letter that will never be delivered.)

Framework: Climax

8 The students agree that they want to do the robbery, which is carried out with great precision and integrity in presentation. The gang returns to headquarters.

Tension: evaluation

Framework: Denouement

9 A roll is called and each man receives the letter which he wrote the day before to his family. The letters are ritually burned, leaving no evidence.

Contrast: all the spectra are in play

Symbol: the gesture of burning
(Collective: we have succeeded.
Individual: I can give them all the things they need; They'll never see me again!; I knew we could do it!)

10 Teacher narration: 'Each man departs one at a time from the safe house with a plane ticket to a foreign land. Concealed in his luggage is his share of the money. He knows that no man may spend even one dollar until six months, at least, have passed. As he waits at the airport, he thinks back over the events of the last three months and of those he is leaving behind and may never see again. He thinks of his confederates and wonders which of them cannot be trusted to obey the laws of the underworld.'
The teacher moves around the room. As she touches each student, he speaks his thoughts so that all may hear.

Contrast: the unpredictable
(There's no such thing as unrestrained freedom.)

Framework: Anagnorisis	**Theatre element**
11 The teacher, out of role, tells the class that as they move to another part of the room and sit down with a partner they become their next of kin (sister, brother, wife, child). 'It is ten months later, there has been no communication. What are your concerns? Begin when you are ready.'	Focus: the family of the robbers Contrast: the unpredictable (No man is an island) Tension: the unknown
12 Discussion: the teacher, using the account of what happened to the money from a robbery in *The Great Train Robbery* (Crichton, 1975),[8] allows the students to draw their own conclusions about bank robbery as a means of earning a living.	Focus: reality Tension: released through knowing that what they did was authentic

The students worked with care, integrity and concern for one another because the teacher accepted their chosen topic. At the same time she fulfilled her educational objectives. She cannot guarantee that these students are all living within the law, though, to this date, she has heard of none who has bungled a bank robbery! The lesson, was, however, a turning point in the students' approach to their work, because they had discovered the satisfaction of moving beyond the plot into the more absorbing world of implications.

Lesson 3

The class had been reading stories of escape. The classroom teacher felt that, although the accounts were autobiographical, the students still regarded the idea of 'hunter' and 'hunted' as an exciting adventure with a happy ending for the 'good guys'.

Many children's games involve, and indeed evolve from, the hunter theme. In the next lesson the teacher chose the game 'Down the Rabbit Hole' as a source for exploring the deeper implications of this theme. A description of this game is given in Appendix 1.

Educational context: Language Arts, Literature
Educational focus: To provide a direct experience which allows the students to understand the difference between escape stories and adventure stories.
Dramatic context: The game, 'Down the Rabbit Hole'
Dramatic focus: The hunter and the hunted

Framework: Exposition	**Theatre element**
1 The teacher tells the students that they are going to do something different in class today. The desks are pushed aside, leaving a clear space in the middle of the room. She explains the rules of the game.	Focus: to understand how to play the game Tension: challenge (to get it right)
2 The students play the game several times with the teacher ensuring that all students have a chance at playing the main roles.	As above
3 The teacher adds a complication: 'This time the game is to be played in silence; only non-verbal signals may be given.'	As above plus the Tension of constraint
4 The students play the game as directed.	As above
Framework: Rising action	
5 The teacher adds a further complication: 'This time, when the hunted is caught, he goes into the nearest 'hole' and sits down. The one he has his back to becomes the quarry as before, the one he faces must sit down with him. The 'hole' or 'safe house' is no longer safe and therefore cannot be used. The Hunter does not change. He must continue the chase. Silence will still be maintained.'	Tension: remains as above for the class, but becomes the Tension of responsibility for the Hunter. Symbolization: the teacher's language begins to change the game into a situation.

Framework: Rising action (cont.)	Theatre element
6 The students play the game with the new rules. After an initial confusion, they begin to think strategically in order to overcome the new constraints.	Focus: shifts to the active players, the Hunter and the Hunted
	Tension: as above
7 The teacher asks a question: 'What was different about this version?' Some answers: 'I didn't like it because I didn't get a chance to play.'	Focus: the students' personal responses to the game.
	Tension: evaluation
'And I didn't like being hunted because, when I was caught, I took someone out of the game with me.' 'Yes, before I wanted the hunted to come so I could play; this time I knew if he did I'd never get to play.' 'I didn't like being the Hunter all the time because everyone was against me.' 'It was easier, though.'	Contrast: from movement and silence to stillness and sound
'No. It was harder because we still couldn't say anything, like 'Go away!' (laughter) 'It was hard work and a different kind of fun.' (general agreement)	Tension: release through laughter
8 The teacher says: 'We'll play the game one more time, and add one more constraint, no-one may run. You can only walk. Be aware of how this changes the situation. Still no speaking, of course.'	Focus: new rules
	Tension: constraint
Framework: Climax	
9 While they play the game, the teacher dims the lights and says: 'Under the cover of darkness, the search continues and the Hunter knows that he has only this night to neutralize the enemy.' When there are only three 'safe houses' left, the teacher brings up the lights. The Hunter, without any	Focus: atmosphere
	Tension: constraints, responsibility
	Contrast: light to darkness
	: peripeteia – the unexpected

Framework: Climax (cont.)	**Theatre element**
instruction, moves to stand behind the teacher. The others remain silent and still.	

Framework: Denouement

10 The teacher, keeping the Hunter beside her, says: 'The rest of you just gather round.'
The students form a loose semicircle and sit down.
'I wonder why all prisoners don't try to escape?'

From this point a wide-ranging discussion follows:
Who is an enemy?
Who are the 'good guys'?
When do you have the right to endanger the safety of innocent people?
What is the difference between courage and foolhardiness?

Focus: to relate their personal experience in the new situation to their intellectual understanding of the literature

Tension: evaluation through reflection

Contrast: from dark to light and silence to sound

Symbolization: the game becomes a metaphor for escape and/or adventure

The quality of the oral discussion carried over into the students' creative writing. It is interesting to note that the tension engendered through the constraint of silence released a flow of spoken and written language which, for the majority of the students, was more expressive and powerful than they had demonstrated in their previous assignments.

Conclusion

Since classroom drama is about 'making it happen' and not about 'what it is' ('what it is' is found in dramatic literature, criticism and theatre history), teachers should acknowledge that the elements of the theatre are as important to their drama work as they are to the playwright and the professional director.

Skill building exercises for teachers

1 Analyze, as we have done above, the lesson 'The sea voyage aboard *The Dreamer*', pp 21–33, from *Dorothy Heathcote: Drama as a Learning Medium* by Betty Jane Wagner, N.E.A., Washington, D.C. (1976).
2 Analyze one of your own drama lessons in the same way.
3 Analyze 'The Way West', pp 37–59, from *Drama Structures* by Cecily O'Neill and Alan Lambert, Hutchinson, London (1982). Look for the break points for each lesson. Can you see a possibility for satisfaction for the students before the end of each lesson?
4 Take time to observe someone else teaching – any subject will do. Note if and how the teacher uses Tension, Contrast, Focus and Symbolization and if the lesson, whatever it is about, follows the structure of the 'well-made play'.

References

1 Wagner, Betty Jane, *Dorothy Heathcote: Drama as a Learning Medium*, p 147
2 Wagner, Betty Jane, *Dorothy Heathcote: Drama as a Learning Medium*, pp 148–158
3 Bolton, Gavin, *Towards a Theory of Drama in Education*, pp 76–78. See also *Drama as Education*, p 92, in which Gavin Bolton identifies the tensions in games as 'reflecting life's common interactions'. We find this list very useful in planning drama
4 Bennett, Stuart, *Drama: The Practice of Freedom*, N.A.T.D., 1984
5 Burke, M. R. and Saxton, J. M., '*A piece of grit*', *London Drama*, 1985
6 Shurtleff, Michael, *Audition*, ch 2, Guidepost 5: Opposites
7 Styan, J. L., *The Drama Experience*, Cambridge University Press, 1965
8 Crichton, Michael, *The Great Train Robbery*, Knopf, New York, 1975

_2_

The two frames of drama

In Chapter 1 we pointed out that teachers should acknowledge the importance of both the elements of the theatre and the structure of the well-made play in planning drama work. The reader might then expect this chapter to be about 'what to do' and 'how to do it'. However, we are putting that on hold because there is an essential to be examined which, in our experience, is rarely considered and which we believe to be fundamental to the achievement of the teacher's educational objectives and the quality of the student's work.

Drama operates in two frames: **the expressive frame** (the outer manifestation) and **the meaning frame** (the inner understanding). However, both students and teacher can get caught up in the external aspects of an activity and scant attention may be paid to that which fuels the expression: the inner world of thought and feeling. The full power of drama can only be realized when the inner world of meaning is harnessed to the outer world of expressive action. Both are, and must be seen as, interdependent. However, expression without meaning is a hollow shell, and meaning must have expressive action in order to ratify itself.

> 'The significance of drama as an expressive form of
> thinking and feeling lies in its concern with the process
> of personal engagement with the objective world.'[1]

Any teacher of drama will recognize that there are different levels of student involvement in the dramatic experience. What are these levels and how can a teacher identify them so that she can promote the kind of work that will bring about a change of understanding which the student can also communicate to others?

A Taxonomy of Personal Engagement

This rather formidable title is simply a definition and extension of Dorothy Heathcote's description of levels of student involvement in the meaning frame:

> 'I must first attract their attention. If I have their
> attention, I can gain their involvement. Then I have a
> chance for their investment and from that their concern.
> If I have their concern, I have hope for obsession.'

We have categorized levels of personal engagement under headings as follows.

- Interest: we have used this term rather than 'attending' because developmental psychologists consider that interest is an emotion in its own right and one of the earliest to appear.
- Engaging: being involved in the task.
- Committing: the development of a sense of responsibility towards the task.
- Internalizing: the recognition of the relationship of the task to the self, revealed as a 'change of understanding'.
- Interpreting: the need to communicate that understanding.
- Evaluating: the willingness to put that understanding to the test.

1   *Interest*

This refers to those components without which drama cannot take place.
1.1 Attending: Because of the process nature of drama, physical presence is imperative.
1.2 Watching: Evidenced by making and maintaining eye contact.
1.3 Listening: Evidenced by congruent, appropriate, supportive verbal response.
1.4 Reacting: Evidenced by congruent, appropriate, supportive non-verbal response.

Since meaning involves thought and feeling, before any learning can take place there must be interest:

- Are they there?
- Are they watching?
- Are they listening?
- Are they responding?

The teacher's function, through her choice of strategies and techniques, is to promote a feeling of curiosity – 'What's next?' If this is present, the teacher can begin to help the students engage in the imaginative world.

2   Engaging

This refers to active identification with imagined roles and situations.

2.1 Acquiescence in being involved: Evidenced by participation in a congruent, appropriate and supportive manner.

2.2 Willingness to engage: Agreement to operate 'as if'; the willing suspension of disbelief.

2.3 Relating: Agreement to accept others, places and objects into the imagined world.

2.4 Identifying: Agreement to endow the role with self, summoning past experience to the demands of the present dramatic situation.

2.5 Evaluating: Satisfaction in the experience.

As you read this, look around. Can you accept your surroundings as the shores of the Pacific? Can you accept yourself as an explorer seeing the great ocean for the first time? Can you think, for a moment, of some of the hardships you have endured in order to reach this prize?

Teachers often need to spend a lot of time working at this level to ensure that the majority of the class are engaged in the imaginative situation and are prepared to endow themselves with the role. The students' satisfaction with their ability to participate in the imagined world generates a feeling of anticipation for what is to come. If that feeling is present, then there is hope for Commitment.

3   Committing

This refers to the acceptance of personal engagement and responsibility to the work and the group: the initial action of empathy.

3.1   Accepting limits: Acquiescence to the drama framework, bound by the limits of the role and the situation.

3.2   Accepting responsibility: Recognition of the transfer of power to the role, with the attendant freedom to disagree or change directions by perceiving consequences and implications.

3.3   Empathizing: Emergence of creative ideas expressed through the attitude and concerns of the role.

Committing does not always follow, even if the students themselves seem to express their willingness for it. In the film *Three Looms Waiting*, the students working with Dorothy Heathcote wanted to do a play about being prisoners of war. Heathcote gets them to agree to be taken prisoner: 'If you want to be in a prison camp, you've got to let me take you there, because there is only one of me and fifteen of you!' Even so, they shot her first time around and she was obliged to reiterate the agreement. It took the boys a long time to realize that the drama demands that they use their power as prisoners against the Commandant, rather than their power as students against the teacher. Heathcote channelling the students' antagonistic feelings against authority into the structure of the drama, so that the inner meaning is congruent with the outward expression that they have chosen, is one of the best examples of good drama teaching that we know of on film.

Once students have allowed themselves to be taken into the play, their creative ideas, attitudes and concerns for the roles are free to emerge. Their intense absorption in the work is apparent and internalization is possible.

4   Internalizing

This refers to the intimate interplay between personal feeling and thought and empathetic feeling and thought.

4.1   Organizing, selecting and ordering according to priorities. Refining values, feelings, concerns, beliefs, attitudes and expectations: submitting them to and making them congruent with the role.

We believe that in art, as in life, there are experiences which occur at the deepest level of our beings for which there are no words at the time. In Internalizing, the student has submitted to the feelings intrinsic to the role. Both he and the teacher will have no difficulty in knowing that a shift in understanding has taken place. Call it 'a moment of truth', 'an aesthetic experience' or 'peak experiencing' (as Mazlow does), we do not need a checklist of behavioural objectives to verify that internalization has occurred.

For example, a class of 12-year-olds was working in a drama in which they had discovered a primitive tribe and were determined to 'educate' them in the ways of the West. After an incident where one of their members and a member of the tribe had been mauled by a jaguar, the westerners held a meeting. Revenge was in the air. The beast, who was being protected by the tribe, must be caught and killed. Amidst the clamour, one boy rose slowly and said: 'There is no place for us here. These primitive people have more concern for life and nature than we have. They understand that the jaguar was in his place and we were intruding.' He turned and walked away. The rest of the class rose as a body and followed him, save for one girl who remained with her head in her hands. Nothing further was said. They were unable to articulate their thoughts and there was no need, at that moment, for words. The teacher quietly suggested that they begin to pack up their equipment. The next day she asked them if they were ready to talk about their experience. She went into role as a concerned member of the group, saying: 'How are we going to explain the apparent failure of our mission?' The 'westerners' chose to write letters to be read by their grandchildren, and the 'natives' to write poems about the jaguar.

Clive Barker has pointed out that in 'The Jaguar', as in so many successful drama lessons, it is precisely when the plot aspects of the 'well-made play' break down that deep learning appears to occur. The teacher, however, maintains the structure of denouement through the action of packing up.

Up to this point in the 'Taxonomy of Personal Engagement', the dramatic activities are spontaneous and explorative. Therefore, there is no product that the teacher can evaluate. She will, however, be able to employ the strategy of Reflection so that the students have an opportunity to examine and synthesize their new understanding and express their satisfaction in the experience. Once there is personal investment (either through Committing or Internalizing), a confidence to communicate this new understanding is generated. This we have called 'Interpreting'.

5   Interpreting

This refers to contextual selection for clarity of communication and not consciously to create theatre.

5.1 Communicating: Listening, observing, judging effect, predicting other points of view, expressing thought and feeling particular to the role.

5.2 Experimenting: Experimenting with expression (voice, gesture, props, etc.) to discover the one which seems most appropriate.

5.3 Adapting: Being ready to consider other ideas; being ready to consider experience outside the self; being ready to negotiate experience to the needs of the role.

5.4 Analyzing: Being willing to analyze feelings by defending a point of view.

5.5 Reflection: Being willing to operate in the reflective mode through spoken or written work, through graphics, physical action or inner reflection.

In Interpreting, the student must be prepared to talk about his feelings, listen to others, experiment with the expression of those feelings and adapt so that other people's feelings may also have expression. He must be confident enough to submit his feelings to analysis.

Working in the second term with a group of adolescents who were in their second year of drama, we began a 'sitting-down' drama. This activity was designed by Gavin Bolton to allow students who do not have much experience to participate in 'making a play' without having to show any action. The students sit on chairs in a circle, taking on roles and talking in the 'as if'. We were making a play on an idea that had appeared during a gift-giving exercise, where the task was to return a gift without giving offence to the giver. 'Jane' had been given an hour-glass because she had such difficulty being on time. She returned it, saying that she had only a few more months to live and did not want a reminder of time, which was now so precious to her. The class chose a number of scenes through which we found out more about Jane, her family, her friends, and her independent outlook. The class decided that the last scene to be explored had to be the scene in the doctor's office. They realized that if the scene was to work, the two who took on the roles of Jane and the doctor would have a very great responsibility. A boy whose father was a doctor volunteered, as he felt he had the kind of experience that would help make the scene real. A girl who had been very quiet for most of the work, said that she thought she could take on the role of Jane. The class turned their chairs away from the two in the scene. What we heard was a good example of this level of the taxonomy. Each student maintained the logic of the story, translating our thoughts and feelings into a spare and honest dialogue. We were all satisfied with the final exchange:

Doctor: Jane, I would like someone to be with you. Shall I call a friend for you?

Jane: Thank-you. No. I would rather go home alone.

The students reflected on their work by writing in role, with everyone writing as Jane, except for the doctor. (For a student's description of this activity, see Appendix 4.)

6   Evaluating

This refers to the testing out of meaning through consciously working in the art form, whether in class or in performance.
6.1 Dramatizing: Selection of appropriate theatrical elements to enhance thought and feeling.
6.2 Symbolizing: Development of symbolic expression to convey significant meaning.
6.3 Monitoring: Detached observation of the effect of action.
6.4 Re-creating: Evidenced by the revitalizing of the technical past by the feeling present.
6.5 Communicating: Satisfaction in the shared significant experience.

Evaluating is the testing out of private feelings in the public forum. The student must be able to express the feelings intrinsic to the role in such a way that the audience will retain them long enough to internalize them. He must deal with the emanations of feeling which the audience returns to him. He must then be able to control his personal response so as to maintain the integrity of the material. In other words, he must not be carried away by the response of the audience into over-acting or over-reacting. How careful we must be in preparing our students to engage at this level!
        At the Ontario Sears Drama Festival after a production of *Canada At War* by a group of twenty high school students, we left for the intermission deeply moved but wondering if it was

simply our ages which had caused us to respond so deeply. We overheard a group of 17 and 18 year olds ahead of us:

'I cried.'
'So did I.'
(Silence)
'That could have been us if we'd been alive.'
(Silence)
'That *was* us. Then.'

Conclusion

We would like to point out that the taxonomy is cumulative. During their drama work, students will not necessarily all be at the same level at the same time, and they may shift back and forth through the levels. However, the students must always progress through the levels in the correct sequence if they are to recapture the appropriate feeling. For example, in a drama lesson[3] where the students were certainly working at level 3 (Commitment), if not at level 4 (Internalization), the drama was at a critical stage where the group was meeting in secret. There was a knock at the door. Could this be a spy? Or worse yet, had they been discovered?

'Answer it!'
'No!'
'It will be more suspicious if we don't answer it and they already know we are in here.'

They slowly opened the door. There stood the Principal who spent the next five minutes discussing administrative matters with the teacher! After he had left, the teacher recognized that she couldn't pick up at the point where the drama had broken off. Her concern was for the quality of the drama. Would it be diminished by the strong evidence of resentment shown by her students at the interruption? She suggested they stop for the day, but they voted unanimously to continue (Interest). She knew she had to re-engage their thoughts and feelings as rebels against the injustice of the times, as opposed to students angry at having their drama spoiled. She took time to go through the task of checking equipment (Engaging) and the ritual of calling the roll (Committing), thus leading her students forward to the point of the interruption. She then skilfully used the real experience of the knock at the door to reinforce the students' awareness of their vulnerability in the imagined world.

A teacher who has planned a lesson with potential for experiencing at level 4 (Internalizing) should be open to opportunities to employ strategies and techniques which will encourage Interpreting and Evaluating. It is the work that students do on these levels which will confirm, both for them and for the teacher, if learning has taken place. A change in understanding can only occur if level 4 has been reached.

Example: The Jaguar (see Internalizing)

Level 1, Interest: 'Let's play "jungle".'

Level 2, Engaging: 'We can teach the natives the proper way to do things.'

Level 3, Committing: 'One of our group has been badly injured. It could happen again. We must do something to prevent another tragedy and the consequent failure of our expedition.'

Level 4, Internalizing: 'It is we who have caused the trouble. This beautiful animal was only doing what was natural. He has never harmed any of the natives. We are the ones who have really made the trouble. We don't know anything about living in this jungle. I'm not sure we could learn.'

Level 5, Interpreting: Individual – The individual expresses his change in understanding in words and actions (5.1). Collective – The individual's words and actions are supported by the actions of the others (5.3); The group finds the appropriate form for retelling the story (5.5).

Level 6, Evaluating: (a) The group share their stories and poems and are satisfied (6.5); (b) The teacher can assess the change in understanding by what is said in the poems and letters and by the quality of thought and feeling behind the expression. In order to verify this change in understanding, the teacher would need to know the students' responses to environmental issues in other subject areas or media.

Up to this point, we have been analyzing **the meaning frame**: the frame that generates, sustains and governs expressive action. We developed the taxonomy in order to understand the levels of feeling that emerge from drama work. When planning work, a teacher can use the taxonomy as a guide to help select strategies and techniques appropriate to the situation. In the lesson itself, the taxonomy operates as a key for choosing techniques to help the students build volume and deepen experience. It also serves as a tool for assessing the progress of the students and their work. This does not mean that **the expressive frame** (that which is seen and heard) is not important. Indeed it is! As we have said before, 'You can't have one without the other'. They are *interdependent*.

Categories of Identification

In a class of thirty students, not all will be able to enter the expressive frame in the same way. This does not mean that a student who lacks expressive skills is not identifying with the dramatic action, simply that he is not able to reveal his thoughts and feelings in a 'showing' way. Also, it does not mean that all that is needed is for him to be shown how to 'show'. This solution results in students spending a lot of time showing how they feel instead of feeling (see Characterizing on page 33).

In order to help teachers recognize the various kinds of student identification in the expressive frame, we have classified student involvement. The five-part classification which follows delineates the increasing complexities of 'becoming someone else'.[2]

1   Dramatic playing
    Being oneself in a make-believe situation.
2   Mantle of the Expert
    Being oneself, but looking at the situation through special eyes.
3   Role playing
    Being in a role representing an attitude or point of view.
4   Characterizing
    Representing an individual lifestyle, which is somewhat or markedly different from the student's own.
5   Acting
    Selecting symbols, movements, gesture and voice to represent a particular individual to others. Acting can be in the form of (a) presenting and (b) performing.

1 Dramatic playing

The student is involved in activities that do not necessarily require him to be anyone other than himself. The activities are designed to place the student in a situation in which he can explore his reactions and actions in a spontaneous way.

For example, the teacher first leads a discussion about pails, water and wells. She then moves her students away from the discussion area towards that part of the classroom where imagination comes into play and where the drama can begin:

> 'Well! Here we are at the top of the hill with our pails and this sign says, "Well condemned by order, City Council". Now what are we going to do?' (She sits exhausted.)

The responses that the students give are many and varied, depending on their personal experiences.

An observer looking at the class might say that the students are in role as 'water carriers', but the stress is on requiring the students to respond as themselves in the situation and not on how they think water carriers would respond.

Much good drama can take place without the students having to walk in any shoes other than their own.

2 Mantle of the Expert

Here the students are working as themselves, but 'as if' they were experts. The role is a general one (we are all engineers, advisors, the tribe, anthropologists . . .), which implies special skills, particular information and/or expertise which can be brought to bear upon the task. There is no definition of individuals and no attitudes are given by the teacher. The pressure is on the dramatic 'here and now' and work is through the task.

For example, the teacher moves the class to a new area and greets them formally:

> 'As members of the Water Board, you are the only people who can solve this problem for us. A fresh water supply is available, but I have no idea how to get it here, how much we'll need or what problems may occur in storing it. Here is a plan of the area and the dimensions of the tanks, which you may find useful in your calculations.'

Here, although still themselves, the students are required to look at the situation through special eyes: those of engineers. This strategy allows the teacher to give up the position of 'the one who knows'. She loses the power of her learning but not the control of the classroom.

3 Role playing

The students are involved here in dealing with a problem where particularization of an attitude or point of view will be one of the means by which the participants will negotiate solutions to the problem. Certain values, either real or deemed suitable for the situation, will be tried out, and the students, seeing that they are protected by the cover of a role, will risk expressing attitudes and points of view which they might not venture in less protected situations.

For example, the teacher welcomes the group into the class-room, and hands out folders marked 'Dr Richardson – Obstetrics, Dr Bedford – Pediatrics, Dr Hirsch – Geriatrics', and so on, thus taking a roll call.

> 'Well, Ladies and Gentlemen, we are going to have to ration the water. As Heads of Departments, I feel it is only fair to involve you in the decisions about which sections of the hospital are to be closed. I recognize that you have been under considerable stress these past few days, but I need not remind you that this hospital has a reputation to uphold. I know it will be difficult for those of you involved in research or with particular patients, but in considering who will go and who will stay, I am sure that you will be thinking of the needs of all. The areas we might look at are the terminal cases, elective surgery, infectious diseases, pediatrics, geriatrics and diagnostics.'

Expertise is implied through the designation of 'Heads of Depart-ments' and made concrete by dissemination of the folders. However, the students, as medical doctors, have a position to defend (not a task to perform as for 'Mantle of the Expert'). It is the 'being' not the 'doing', and the 'me' is often suppressed in the interests of the role. It is the first stage in the transfer from identification as self to identification as performer.

4 *Characterizing*

Characterization has been described as 'the outer clothing of the inner life'. It is the communication of a representation of a life-style, and should not consciously be to create a theatrical effect. This is where students often think they should begin their drama work. These students tend to show a stereotyped interpretation of the role – hand-wringing misers, shushing librarians – because they have not had the opportunity, through working in some or all of the first three categories, to find the person inside the role.

Students who have been role-playing will begin to characterize as a means of expressing more fully their inner thoughts and feelings. The emotional context of the situation, or the information in a source, or the need to affect others, or the situation itself, will impel students into characterization.

For example, a teacher working with a class of ten-year-olds interested in a royal visit decided to look at what goes on behind the scenes. Using the story of *Cinderella* as a source, the students, in the Mantle of the Expert as cooks, are preparing the wedding banquet of the Prince and Cinderella. The teacher, as head cook, puts the pressure on by stating that both time and money are limited but they will be expected to do a good job. If they over-spend or are not ready on time, they may lose their jobs. If the meal is not up to standard, their reputations as the best cooks in the land will be lost. By presenting them with this dilemma, she hopes they will move into role.

There is much discussion. The teacher, using Narration (see Chapter 5, page 142), sums up the relevant arguments. This focuses their attention on the real problem which is, 'What are we going to do?' The students decide they want to see the man at the top, and ask for an interview with the Chamberlain. The teacher, in role as the go-between, points out the implications: Are they prepared to walk out, to continue to work under unsat-isfactory conditions, to face dismissal for insubordination? As teacher she suggests they practise what they will say and how they will approach the Chamberlain. Here she is moving them into Characterizing.

The students work in pairs: one as cook and one as Chamber-lain. The teacher moves from group to group, watching, listening, asking questions, making suggestions to help them maintain the attitudes and feelings of the role while they are experimenting with stance, gesture and voice. She is not looking for consistency because in Characterizing the student must be free to explore the external manifestations of the role in order to discover those which are most effective for him. The cooks then choose someone to represent them and, in a simulation interview, they act as critics, the 'appointee' incorporating their suggestions.

When the Chamberlain (School Librarian as 'stranger in role', see Chapter 5, page 148) arrives, he is met by the cooks, and their representative states their case clearly and confidently. What we are seeing is the natural, visible extension of the role. Up to this point we have seen the student in role but now we begin to hear and see the role itself.

5   Acting

The fifth category has two facets: **presenting** and **performing**. We make this distinction deliberately in order to accommodate two kinds of theatrical product which occur in a school situation. We believe, from our experience, that this differentiation is also valid in the professional theatre; thus, presentation is to performance as workshop productions and on the road try-outs are to fully established productions.

In **presenting**, the orientation is still process, for the product itself is an element of the process; a necessary learning step before performance. The focus for the teacher is the satisfaction of those involved in 'the making of the play'.

In **performing**, the orientation is to the product and the focus for the students and the teacher is the satisfaction of the audience.

When acting, in either presentation or performance, the student must be able to convey subtleties of nuance and gesture, to 'read', use, and work with the energy of the audience, and to maintain a high degree of energy himself. Along with communicating the inner life of the character and the meaning and implications within the play itself, the actor is working in all these categories:

- being himself in an imagined situation
- seeing with the special eyes of the character
- expressing the attitudes and points of view of the character
- representing that character to the audience
- monitoring the whole of the performance, himself included, so that it is clean and clear.

The skill of acting is to transfer what is happening on stage to the audience in such a way that they see only the character and not the person who is playing the character.

As in the Taxonomy of Personal Engagement, students who have been working in any of the first four Categories of Identification have been doing so in a spontaneous and explorative fashion, and may shift back and forth through the categories, depending upon their interest in the situation and their involvement in the work. The teacher has to enable the processes of both Identification and Engagement to happen, and not just expect them to happen naturally.

The fifth category, Acting, is a restrictive and highly disciplined activity in which the student is confined to the secondary processes of creativity and is no longer free to shift around spontaneously. What will save this work from becoming rote representation (full of 'sound and fury signifying nothing') are the strategies and techniques used by the teacher in rehearsal and the student's own ability to maintain the vitality of his engagement with the meaning frame.

Conclusion

All this may seem rather formidable but these categories can be observed in children's play. Ten children, ranging in age from 7 to 12 years, were playing 'Jaws' in a swimming pool. The game involved a catcher, 'Jaws' the shark, pursuing the rest of the group. If he could hold any portion of another child's body in his two hands, that child was assumed to be eaten and therefore out of the game. A couple of the children never really joined the game at all, swimming at the edges of the pool and keeping out of the way (no involvement in the imagined world, but not making an issue of it). One or two accepted that when they were caught they had been 'eaten' (Category 1, dramatic playing). Another child announced that he had 'anti-shark serum' so he could not be caught (Category 2, Mantle of the Expert). Three were busy helping the less-experienced and planning avoidance tactics (Category 3, Role playing). 'Jaws' himself circled in a menacing fashion humming the *Jaws* signature tune (Category 4, Characterizing). 'Dad', one cried, 'Come and watch us play "Jaws" ' (Category 5, Acting).

The drama was exciting and involving, and all the children contributed to the whole dramatic experience in their own way.

Summary

We have now illustrated the six levels in the Taxonomy of Personal Engagement in the meaning frame and the five Categories of Identification in the expressive frame. They do not necessarily run parallel to one another, for a student may well be at the Commitment level while operating in the Mantle of the Expert, and many of us have seen 'professionals' operating in the Acting category when they can barely generate interest for themselves, let alone for their audience!

The drama teacher is responsible for the smooth interaction of both frames for:

- the individual student, so that his inner meaning is congruent with his outer expression.
- the individual student and the group, so that the student's two frames are operating in a way which corresponds with the two frames of the class.
- the class, so that the agreed meaning is expressed through appropriate collective action.

Teachers who understand these classifications, whether in classroom exploration or theatre presentation, are better able to select strategies and techniques which engender a richer *expressive* frame woven together with a more deeply felt and intellectually significant *meaning* frame. The two invaluable techniques which a teacher has at her disposal for the interweaving of expression and meaning are her skills in questioning and her ability to work in role.

Skill building exercises for teachers

1 Analyze 'The Haunted House', Chapter 7, pages 167–171, in *Drama Structures*: (a) Make a graph of the Levels of Personal Engagement you think were achieved by the students, (b) Insert on the graph the appropriate Category of Identification for each level.

2 Choose one of your own role dramas, list the Levels of Personal Engagement, Categories of Identification and the intellectual demands, as we have done in 'Three Poor Tailors' at the end of Chapter 4.

References
1   Bolton, Gavin, *Towards a Theory of Drama in Education*, p 20, 1979
2   For comparison see Callow, Simon, *Being an Actor*, Part Two, Methuen, London, 1984
3   Teacher: Alexandra Lucas, Grade 8, St. Martin's Elementary School, Smithville, Ontario, 1984

_3

Teacher in role

> The most significant kind of learning which is
> attributable to experience in drama is a growth in the
> pupils' understanding about human behaviour,
> themselves and the world they live in. This growth of
> understanding, which will involve changes in customary
> ways of thinking and feeling, is likely to be the primary
> aim of drama.[1]

In role play the participants see the world through someone else's eyes and in so doing not only show the outer aspects of that person, but also try to understand how that person thinks and feels.

Students engage in role play in their dramatic play, in exercise and when they work in script, but these activities are often subsumed in the strategy of a role drama. A role drama uses a context to provide a structure for the students' exploration (see page 119).

In a role drama, the most effective teaching technique is that of teacher in role. Here the teacher is 'taking a part in the play' and at the same time monitoring the experiences of her students. Her most important role is that of teacher, controlling class discipline and learning but releasing the power to the students when they are ready.

For example, a pre-school child in his own dramatic play is conducting traffic as if he were a policeman. As his mother approaches, he slips out of role to say, 'Look, Mum, I'm a policeman.' His mother has many ways of responding:

- 'No, you're not. You're Johnny.' (Denying the role.)
- 'So you are, dear.' (Placating the child.)

- 'Why don't you wear the policeman's hat?' (Adding to the externals of 'policeman'.)
- 'A policeman directs traffic this way.' (Giving skills but no new understanding of 'policeman'.)
- 'Sir, could you please tell me how to get to the hospital?'

In the last response the mother takes on a role and in doing so is:

- accepting the situation and guiding the child back into role where he is still in charge.
- upgrading language (formal mode of address).
- upgrading the job ('Sir').
- giving opportunities for the child to accept the fact that a policeman has a respected and responsible job, not only directing traffic but helping the citizens of the community in many ways.

As a second example, a group of 16-year-old students are working on an improvisation where one student is interviewing another for a job as a guide on an expedition. One pair is obviously working superficially. The teacher could say: 'Mary and Michael, stop fooling and get on with it or go away and sit down!'. Alternatively, she can adopt a role saying: 'The leader of the expedition does not want it to fail because of an unskilled and uncommitted team. Are we wasting our time interviewing this candidate. I wonder why he ever applied for the job?' By taking a role, the teacher is:

- guiding Mary and Michael into role.
- reinforcing the task and upgrading the language.
- enriching the material and reminding them of their previous commitment.

Teaching stances

In the drama classroom, the teacher is in there teaching, always engaged in the action, sometimes covertly, sometimes overtly. Drama is not a subject that can be 'phoned in'. An observer may see a teacher working as one of the following:

Manipulator

This is the traditional instructive stance when the teacher gives information to the student. Generally the students are physically inactive, though listening (she hopes!). 'Manipulator' has unpleasant connotations in teaching. However, we accept ourselves as manipulators, for the *Oxford English Dictionary* defines it as 'one who handles or treats with skill'.

Facilitator

This is the stance of those teachers working in subject areas where practice is an important component of student learning. The teacher is moving amongst the students offering help, or the students are coming to the teacher as a resource person. 'Facilitator' may suggest making things easy, but it is defined as 'promoting or helping forward'. As teachers, we accept this as our purpose.

Enabler

This is a less used but historically valid stance where the teacher is inside the work as one who is learning with her students. 'Enabler' is defined as 'one who empowers a person with the means to do'. In the United Kingdom, the Enabling Act of 1920 conferred on the established church (the class) a certain measure of autonomy, subject to parliamentary veto (the teacher and the rules of the game). As teachers we accept this as the basis of our philosophy.

All three stances are appropriate in the drama classroom, and all three can be used effectively in or out of role. Each stance carries within it implications of status: the teacher's position on the ladder of power in relation to her students. A role of *high status*, for example, implies a high degree of threat for those below that rank, great responsibility and high risk for the one who wields the power. *Middle status* allows the teacher to hand over some responsibility and to draw it back if the students are eager only for the privileges of leadership and not the responsibilities. *Low status*, on the other hand, puts the teacher at risk, unless, as stated at the beginning of this chapter, she is, through her role, monitoring and helping the class to be aware of the implications of their decisions and actions. When used skilfully, a low status role can provide an excellent means of injecting tension without intervening in the students' work. Cecily O'Neill uses this very effectively in her work (see Chapter 4, page 81). Whatever status or stance the teacher takes, she must learn to recognize the potential for formulating meaning from what might seem an insignificant moment to the student.

Advantages of the teacher taking a role

- The teacher is within the drama and can view *with* the class, what is happening.
- She is controlling the pace and tension because she is in touch with the internal rhythm of the work.
- She can support and encourage, keeping the lines of communication open, so all can work within a consensus.
- She has the opportunity to share discovering with her students and to move with them into new understanding.

There are also advantages for the students when the teacher takes a role.

- It provides opportunities for them to take responsibility, make decisions, and assume the leadership of the group.
- It provides the freedom to express attitudes and points of view within the safety of the role.
- It gives them the excitement of challenging the teacher with confidence. For example:

    'When I was the owner of the Pet Shop, I could say what I felt when I argued with you as the Minister of Health, but it's hard to do that when you are the teacher and they (peers) are listening to me as me.'

    student (aged 10)

Teaching roles for a teacher in role

In the theatre, if you ask an actor what role he is playing, he is more likely to answer with the name, rather than the function, of the character ('Henry V' rather than 'the one in charge'). In educational drama, what is important is the function of the role in both the dramatic interaction and in stimulating learning. In the analysis which follows, we identify nine teaching roles and look at the advantages, disadvantages and the potential learning for students. Each role description is illustrated by four role drama contexts and the suggested roles a teacher might take.

1   Role: Authority
Status: high
Stance: Manipulator

Description: The teacher is in charge with full authority and is overtly in control. She is the 'one who knows' and the class is aware of this.

Advantages: As it is similar to the traditional teacher role, the teacher feels comfortable and the students secure. It is easy for the teacher to control the pace and tension. However, it is possible to move within the role to a stance in which authority may be relinquished for a little while in order to see how the students handle more responsibility.

Disadvantages: There is little opportunity for the class to take responsibility or make group decisions. It is difficult for a leader to emerge unless the teacher relinquishes her power. There is always the danger of 'kill the king'. The Tension is often in the real rather than in the imagined world. (See Chapter 1, page 3.)

Potential learning: language skills; discovering the rules of the game; experiencing interaction with authority in a different guise; authority roles can receive new information. On the simplest level, this will involve the students in explaining, demonstrating, suggesting, advising, supporting, etc.

Examples
A convent: The Mother Superior
A hospital (surgical wing): Chief Surgeon
A kingdom: The King, The Queen
A space ship: Head of NASA (operations)

2   Role: Second in Command
Status: middle
Stance: Manipulator, Facilitator, Enabler

Description: The teacher is the 'go-between.' She doesn't know but offers to find out. She is not overtly in control but may refer to a higher authority for instructions.

Advantages: The flexibility of the role allows the teacher, at any time, to relinquish authority or take full authority as the situation demands. She is protected from 'kill the king' as she shares the class problem. The class must make some decisions and take some responsibility with the opportunity for a leader to emerge. Control of pace and tension is still in the hands of the teacher. The tension tends to move into the imagined world.

Disadvantages: There are few, but the teacher must avoid slipping into full authority or allowing the class to force her into the role of the authority who makes decisions.

Potential learning: appropriate language; problem-solving skills; independent thinking; language skills; awareness of the art of questioning; the importance of making the right decisions.

Examples
The convent: a senior member of the Council (Bursar, Choir Mistress)
The hospital: a senior doctor
The kingdom: The Chancellor
The space ship: The Captain

3   Role: One of the Gang
Status: low
Stance: Enabler

Description: Authority is not overtly in the hands of the teacher but she can keep control by questions and suggestions. She knows no more than the class, but, unlike Second in Command, she is unsure where to find the facts or to whom to go. Her opinions should carry no more weight than those of her students, and she makes use of 'we' and 'us' when speaking of 'our' plans.

Advantages: The teacher is one with the class and can suggest and question on their level. The class can be led into making decisions, taking responsibility and assuming leadership. The teacher still controls the pace and tension through questioning. The class will have an opportunity of seeing the teacher in a different light. The tension is half in the real and half in the imagined world.

Disadvantages: The teacher needs confidence (in herself and the class) in order to relinquish her authority. She must be seen to respect the authority of the leader who is chosen by the class or who chooses to take responsibility. She must be prepared to accept what the class gives. She is on a tight-rope without a net!

Potential learning: The class may use listening skills, questioning skills, problem-solving skills. The class may become aware of the difficulties involved in working with authority; the importance of listening to each other; the importance of choosing the right leader; the importance of making the right decisions.

Examples
The convent: a young professed nun
The hospital: a doctor or nurse
The kingdom: a member of the Court
The space ship: an astronaut

4 Role: The Helpless
Status: very low
Stance: Enabler

Description: The teacher is now in the hands of and sometimes at the mercy of the class. She *needs* their help, doesn't know and depends upon the class to find out. Her questioning and comments may feed in clues. She still has her standards and can refuse by saying 'I don't think I could do that.'

Advantages: The responsibility, decision-making and leadership are now with the class, though at no time is the class discipline out of her control. She can assess the abilities of the class from within. Tension is one-quarter in the real world and three-quarters in the imagined.

Disadvantages: As for role 3, the teacher needs confidence in the class, in herself and in the relationship between them. It is often difficult to withhold knowledge and the role must be one that demands concern from the students.

Potential learning: The class may use language skills; questioning skills; problem-solving skills. The class may become aware of their values; the implications of their actions on another person; the importance of giving clear instructions and relevant information, and of non-verbal signals.

Examples
The convent: a postulant/novice

The hospital: a patient
The kingdom: a serf
The space ship: a trainee

5   Role: Authority Opposed to the Group
Status: high
Stance: Manipulator (overt), Enabler (covert)

Description: Differs from role 1 in that the teacher is not the authority *over* the group, but one from another group who challenges them. The class must know the rules of the 'game' of drama. The choice of role must be appropriate. A spaceman in a convent might cause the wrong kind of difficulties, but the man who is looking for his prize pumpkin in *Cinderella* has possibilities!

Advantages: The class is in charge of itself. The teacher can increase or relieve the pressure when appropriate. The teacher is in a position to challenge the group and the individual. Tension tends to be in the imagined world.

Disadvantages: The teacher, through her high status role, must be sensitive to the ability of the class to work as one group and their ability to accept the leader who emerges. 'Kill the king' is a danger unless the rules of the game are understood and accepted by all.

Potential learning: The class may use language skills; questioning skills; debating skills. The class may experience working under pressure; respecting their own authority; opposition to their authority. The class may become aware of the necessity of accepting authority for the good of the group; the problems of control of language under stress.

Examples
The convent: The Bishop
The hospital: The Investigative Commissioner
The kingdom: a republican
The space ship: an alien

6   Role: Devil's Advocate
Status: high
Stance: Manipulator

Description: The teacher is a member of the group but challenges the decisions of the group largely through tone of voice, facial expression and physical attitude. Her challenges must be strong and she must be prepared to support these challenges.

Advantages: Similar to those of role 5 as the pressure on the class is to withstand. This role gives a good opportunity for the class to defend its ideas and decisions, for leaders to emerge and for a strong commitment to the task to be built.

Disadvantages: As for role 5 but the teacher must make sure that her opposition does not make the class crumble and accept her ideas, thus turning her into Authority. The teacher must ensure that her role is logical and her advocacy sound, and that she has a right to belong to the group.

Potential learning: As for role 5, but with the subtle difference that the teacher is a *bona fide* member of the group. This membership permits her to question and comment on 'personal' role concerns and feelings.

Examples
The convent: a novice mistress
The hospital: a surgeon with a new technique
The kingdom: a rebel
The space ship: an astronaut who has lost faith in the purpose
                            of the voyage

7   Role: The Absentee
Status: middle
Stance: Enabler

Description: The teacher can be in any one of roles 1, 2, 3 or 6, entering as one of the group who has been absent for a while and so 'doesn't know'. She must draw information from the class as to what has happened in her absence. For example, 'What did you decide while I was away?' Note that the teacher does not actually leave the classroom but is out of role and inconspicuous. She may or may not hear what the class is planning.

Advantages: Gives an opportunity to slow down the action in an action-oriented class. This role provides more than an opportunity for checking memory. The dialogue may become a form of reflection, prompted by appropriate questioning from the teacher.

Disadvantages: The teacher must accept the information provided by the class even though she knows it is inaccurate and may have difficulty suppressing her own knowledge of the facts. She may, however, doubt: 'Are you sure?', 'Do you all agree?'

Potential learning: The class may use language skills and teaching skills. The class may experience recalling and presenting incidents; reliving what has happened; reflecting on the experience and its implications; supporting the group's decisions; supporting others in the group.

Examples
The convent: someone who has been training at another convent
The hospital: an old surgeon visiting after retirement
The kingdom: a crusader
The space ship: Mission Control (debriefing)

8 Role: Authority Outside the Action
Status: high/middle
Stance: Facilitator

Description: The teacher is usually an administrator who will be at the service of the group but the initiative comes from the group. She is there to advise when requested to do so and to ensure that all groups are working to the same focus.

Advantages: The teacher is an observer but can control the action by opposing the easy solution and ensuring that all groups, or members of the group, are working and involved in the dramatic activity.

Disadvantages: The teacher has little control over the learning as the class tends to move into its own dramatic play and does not need her. It is often difficult to find a way in without reverting to an authority role.

Potential learning: The class may use listening skills; speaking skills; technical language. The class may experience self-directed learning; learning from peers; using authority effectively.

Examples
The convent: The Reverend Mother/The Mother General
The hospital: The Administrator
The kingdom: The Chamberlain
The space ship: The Co-ordinator

9   Role: The fringe role
Status: high/middle
Stance: Facilitator

Description: Here the teacher is in no specific role except of one who has the right to be there and to ask questions. It is used primarily to help the class build background and sometimes as a control when the class is working in groups and when the teacher wants to know what is happening.

Advantages: Because of the vagueness of the teacher's role, she appears to have no vested interest in the central dilemmas of the situation, so there are opportunities for expressing personal thoughts and feelings. The role allows the teacher to deepen the understanding or slow the action without being in full role. The class has the opportunity to put the teacher into a role if that makes them feel more comfortable, but generally they accept the intervention without requiring a specific 'who'.

Disadvantages: It is sometimes confusing if the teacher is not careful in her choice of questioning techniques. She then becomes an interrogator. It may delay commitment if the teacher has not warned the class that she may move in, in role. The teacher must not be caught without a role up her sleeve or the drama may turn into 'What is this spy doing here?'

Potential learning: The class may use language skills through listening and answering questions. They may gain experience of building commitment through the teacher's intervention. They may become aware of the necessity of holding role.

Examples
(The role you take will depend upon the activity, we make the following suggestions as guides.)
The convent: a confessor; The Extern Sister, who deals with the outside world in a cloistered order; a lay sister
The hospital: receptionist, clerk, nurse, cleaning lady
The kingdom: The Minstrel, a messenger, a courtier
The space ship: If the class is *on* the space ship, you cannot suddenly appear! You can fulfill a fringe role as the radio communicator, media interviewer or statistician, on the ground.

When a teacher takes on a role it does not mean that she is allowing the class to get out of her control. The discipline of the normal classroom and the rules of the game will be kept. Once inside the drama, the teacher has given up the power but *not* responsibility for the class or the work. The power of the situation and the tensions within it produce their own discipline.

Some questions teachers have asked

What happens if the class stops seeing me as teacher?
- Is it not a good thing for your students to see other aspects of your personality?
- If discipline is what you are concerned about, take a role where it would be logical for you to maintain discipline. However, the class may find it difficult to separate your drama role from your teacher role: reiterate 'I am in role now.'
- Students need to be introduced to 'teacher in role' gradually. Naturally, if you start off as The Helpless they may take advantage!
- Designate a chair as an 'out of role' gathering place.
  'I shall be taking a part in the play with you. Whenever I come to sit on this chair I shall want you to stop what you are doing. It means that I want to talk to you as your teacher.'[2]
  This silent signal for out of role work is quite different from the drum or 'freeze' which you may have used in P.E. or games. Often the actual activity of moving between the 'drama space' and the chair and back to the drama space gives time for the students to change from imaginative play to the 'real' world.

I cannot act. How can I take a role?
- Please *don't* act! The teacher must remember that the class is not her audience. It is not you as performer or entertainer that is important, but the learning which your role can stimulate.
- In role playing, if you recall the Categories of Identification (Chapter 2), you are simply required to represent an attitude or point of view. It is the internal communication which is important (see page 32 for elaboration).

When I start role playing should I lose all sense of 'self' and become immersed in that 'other'?
- Certainly not! The teacher's eye and ear must monitor what is going on, how time is passing and if the educational objectives are being met. You are not a method actor!

How do I go into role?

- It is important that both you and the students have a very clear moment for the beginning of the role drama.

  'I think we are ready to start now. I am going to leave you for a moment. When I come back I shall speak to you as if I were somebody else and our play will begin.'

  The walk away provides a certain tension, and if the discussion leading up to this moment has not indicated the teacher's role, the tension will be heightened by a sense of mystery.

- Remember that when in role in a role drama everything is moving in the present tense and you and your students are part of the here and now. Drama, as James Moffett describes it, is 'What *is* Happening'.[3]

If I'm in role how can I evaluate?

- If you are in it you will find, with experience, that it is very easy to recall what you did and even what was said. Make time to jot notes after class. Reflective work by students, in or out of role, is often a good means of confirming your impressions (See Chapter 7 on Evaluation).

Can I come out of role but leave the students in role?

- Of course you can, and it is often a very good thing to do. You may feel that it is time for them to get on on their own; you may want to see if they can structure the drama for themselves; you may wish to change roles or you may need some time to gather your thoughts about where to go next. For whatever reason, you can withdraw in a number of ways, for example by saying, 'I can't stay around here, I'm needed elsewhere' or by building into the role a reason for leaving: 'I will take your decision back to the authorities.'

There's only one of me. How can I change roles without confusing the students?

- Isn't that what drama is all about? The difficulty will be if you change the outward 'look' of the role but keep the same inner attitude or expect the same respect. When the initial role is no longer appropriate it is important to move to another one. The students will have no difficulty in accepting a change of role if you have signalled clearly that a change has taken place. Students get confused when a teacher changes from, say, Authority to Absentee and then says, 'No, no. You've got it all wrong!'

- If you know what learning you can promote by changing roles you should have no difficulty.

How do I change role?

- By saying: 'I'm going to change roles now. I'm going to walk away and when I come back I will be . . . . . .' or 'You will know who I am.'
- By leaving the playing space: 'You've not heard the last of me!' and coming back immediately: 'Whoever that was was certainly in a bad temper! What's happened in here?'
- You can leave something behind that your previous role had used. It may simply remain as a representation or as a symbol, depending on its 'weight', or you can refer to it: 'Look at this list of demands from The Queen'.

When do I stop the role drama?

The teacher should be in control of when to stop, not the bell! But stopping does not only occur at the end of a lesson.

Stopping in the middle

Teachers, like radio announcers, do not like 'dead air'. They tend to push on even when nothing is being accomplished. The stop in the middle of a lesson is often regarded by inexperienced teachers as an admission of personal failure. But in role drama, the teacher and the students share the responsibility for the action. It is the 'teaching eye' of the teacher which the students should be able to rely upon to stop things:

- when there is a need to sum-up before going on
- when you have used inappropriate strategies, activities or techniques
- when you are not satisfied with the standard of work
- when you have achieved your lesson objectives
- when there is nothing new to be discovered in the situation (This is very hard, as it is often when things are going well

that you want to relax and enjoy it – but you must not indulge
yourself!)
- when the expressive action (plot) has taken over from the
inner meaning
- when you are not sure what is going on: 'Let's stop and see
what we have.'
- when being in role is not being very effective. It is far better
to come out of role clearly and positively than to pursue it
against hopeless odds. 'Right. Stop for a moment.'
- when a disintegrating role drama can be turned into a group
discussion which will provide a valuable reflection upon the
content and issues of the lesson.

It takes sensitivity. Although there is no great harm in letting
something that is working well go on, the rule when doing
role drama is that it is better to stop short than to let them
wallow.

Stopping at the end of the period
Each lesson should have the same structure as the well-made
play (see Chapter 1), but this is sometimes difficult to ensure in
a role drama. Some things the teacher can say when the drama
is not finished are: 'What do we need to do in order to feel that
we have finished today?', 'Where shall we go next drama period?'

How do I finish a role drama?
- Sometimes a role drama will have a natural conclusion that
you and the students recognize as entirely satisfying.
- There are times when for one reason or another you will
want or need to stop the drama. You can then:
  (a) Ask the students 'What scene must we have in order to
  finish our work?' or 'What must happen if we are to know
  how things work out for these people?'
  (b) Ask them to write the end of the story individually, or as
  a group might see it.
  (c) Synthesize the main points of the story and suggest a
  conclusion as a stimulus for reflection.

It is important to recognize when the role drama is complete,
that is, when there is nothing further for the students to learn;
when they have lost interest; when the teacher's objectives

have been met (but not before the students are satisfied by their work).

How do I deal with what the students give me?
- First of all, you know why you have chosen your role.
- You have done some thinking and research on the role, so the background is available to you.
- You are really listening to what is being said (and are not busily planning something wonderful to happen next!)
- There is no reason at all why you should not say, 'I'm not sure what we should do next. Has anyone an idea?'
- It is perfectly all right for you to say, 'I'm going to have to think about that for a minute', and then do so. Students are often surprised and interested to watch their teacher think!

Students often know better than the teacher how to deal with a problem and enjoy working out a solution. There is no rule in drama that says that the teacher must know all the answers and the role of 'the one who does not know' is an excellent stimulus to learning.

How can I find the time to fit role drama into the curriculum?
- Look at the syllabus. It is our experience that it suggests *what* you teach but not *how* to teach it. Role drama is one way of teaching select areas of the curriculum where the relationship between human beings is paramount. If you are a teacher who believes that concepts, ideas, creative solutions and implications are valuable components of teaching and learning then you cannot leave role drama out of your teaching. Facts and dates also fit easily into this kind of teaching, because they have a context of experience on which to hang.

Problems of the class when the teacher is in role

Role is a powerful medium and there are general behaviour roles which the students can take and which present problems for the teacher. These problems can be found in an individual, a small group or the whole class.

The Spaghetti Western

This is when the group or an individual is concerned with the plot action: 'and then . . . and then . . . and then . . .' The approach is very common when students are first introduced to drama. They have been brought up on television programmes which are plot-oriented, or computer games which are action-oriented. They think drama is about *what* happens. The teacher must satisfy this expectation, but, at the same time, she must find a way to slow the action by examining each episode and what happens between the episodes. Drama is about *why* things happen.

> It is not how the man was killed, but what drove us to do it.
>
> Dorothy Heathcote, *Three Looms Waiting*

See Chapter 5 for techniques to 'slow down' the drama.

Kill the King

This is evidenced by something very dramatic happening which is a surprise for the teacher and often for the rest of the class!

For example, in *Rumplestiltskin*, the Lord Chamberlain (a student) suddenly has a heart attack. The probable reason is that the student thinks he is expected to make something happen (see Spaghetti Western). The way to handle the situation is to ask the class in which direction they wish to go: 'Stop. Do we want to solve the problem of the Queen giving up her baby, or do we want to investigate why the Lord Chamberlain has fainted?'

In *The Factory* the foreman (the teacher) is locked out of the factory by the workers. The probable reason is that the students want to 'get the teacher' for some reason. Obviously the class does not want you at this time, so here is an opportunity to find out how they manage on their own: 'Stop. Now that you no longer trust the foreman, have you thought how you will solve the problem of the lay-offs?' Note that you are not saying 'Now that you no longer trust *me*'.

In *Refugees* a small group of students take charge by mowing down their companions, effectively putting an end to the drama for those who have died! The probable reason is that the students are bored, or have lost the focus and are desperate for action. You need to hear from both the action-takers and those against whom the action has been taken: 'Stop. Do we want to try and understand what it is like to leave your homeland unseen? We can cancel what has happened (the mowing-down). Or do we want to find out how stress causes a group to fall apart? In either case we must go back in time.'

The Monopolizer

This can be one student or a small group and can take the following forms:
(a) The one who picks up the situation quickly and moves into role before any of the others are ready. The teacher must not ignore or put this student down. He can be silenced, but his importance must be kept. For example (in role): 'You are the obvious leader of this group, but I would like to hear from the others, too.' Or out of role: 'Don't waste your ideas too early. Hold back a little and wait to see what happens.' If the context is appropriate, you can isolate the Monopolizer, putting him where the class can still see him as 'hero', for example, he is silenced for his beliefs.

It is important for both the Monopolizer and for the rest of the group that everyone has an opportunity to contribute. The former will discover that others have ability too, and the latter must have a chance to take some responsibility for the drama.
(b) This is the student who is looking for attention because he is not popular. The class will often take care of this for you! They make their personal feelings relevant in the context of the drama. For example, a group of students in Mantle of the Expert were investigating a community where everyone had died and were irritated by someone who ostentatiously left the discussion at an important information time and walked about the imaginary dead bodies. The group isolated him, their reason being that he might have been contaminated as no-one yet knew the cause of death. The teacher left him isolated for a while, reintegrating him when the drama had moved on.

If the class is unable to deal with the problem in context, the teacher must do so. Here are some other suggestions:

- In or out of role she can employ him in a role which he will see as important, but gives him no opportunity for irritating the rest of the class, for example, The Keeper of the Sword.
- Pair him with a student who is strong enough to withstand the residue of his unpopularity. Be sure to acknowledge this student's contribution privately when possible.

- Talk to the student. He can often see the solution to his problem and only needs your support and advice.
- Drama works through the collective. If the student continues to draw focus to himself, it may be in the best interests of everyone, including the student, to arrange for a transfer.

The Comedian

He, or they, are the one(s) who turn every situation into a comedy, sometimes inside the drama and sometimes by side-comments or actions. The reason may be that the student is the class comic and is merely fulfilling his role in the class, or that he wants attention, or that he is bored.

The comedian has to be a good comic to make it work, and he is under constant pressure to maintain his role. He becomes a problem when his comic role overrides his dramatic role. Our favourite examples:

Teacher: 'And where did you find the secret message?'
Student: 'In my lady's drawers, my lord.'
or
Teacher: 'And how did you open the chest?'
Student: 'With my lord's tool, your honour.'

It's a wonderful joke so 'Stop and let's all laugh' and then move on. Don't go over it to get it right or you will all go on laughing at the same spot! On the other hand, the funny line can be handled by the teacher in role, reiterating the seriousness of the matter: 'You don't seem to realize the seriousness of the matter.'

If the only role the student can play is the Comedian, you should speak to him privately and challenge him to try other roles and be sure to reprimand the class if they are expecting him to be funny and are egging him on: 'I thought you had agreed to work here as adults.' Be sure to give the student lots of teacher support when he is trying to work in some other role.

The Spoiler

Unlike the student above, this one is out to spoil the drama. He will do it from the outside, not coming into the drama but making comments from the periphery about the other students' work. The solution here may be: 'Out! You are not interested or ready for this work!' Alternatively, he may do it from the inside, where he apparently accepts the role and the situation, but his words and actions are clearly out of context. The answer here may be: 'Out! You are not yet mature enough for this work.'

In both cases make it easy for his re-entry by adding: 'When you are ready, you may rejoin us.'

This arrangement must be cleared with the administration. Say you are trying something that demands concentration from all and you suspect that the student is not willing to work at that level. We have never yet met an administrator who was not supportive.

Do not be soft about all this, any more than you would be with a disruptive student in any other subject. You are teaching 30 students and if one messes it up, get rid of him for a while and educate the rest. 'Function in disaster. Finish in style!'

The Actor

This is the student who has taken acting classes and performed in many plays where the emphasis has only been on the expressive frame. He demonstrates 'how it should be done'. He is also heard, or seen, correcting his peers. His expectation will be in terms of performance and presentation and he decries the work in role because he sees no purpose for it. These students can be a problem because they are operating as critics and directors at an inappropriate time.

The solution might be to:

- ignore this over-demonstration and hope that the student will realize that this is not what is wanted.
- remind the student that this work is a different order of experience and he must use his 'expertise' in another way. This takes great tact, forbearance and firmness.
- state bluntly that you do not believe in what was done or said and that even professional actors have to work very hard to find their own way to express the truth.

The gifted child

This is the natural role player who has the taste and the ability to make the right choices and the power to allow us to perceive them. He knows intuitively what to do and it seems to come so easily that he may not feel sufficiently challenged. Be grateful and find ways of challenging him. Do not simply give the responsibility for the drama to him and sit back yourself. Gavin

Bolton has a nice illustration of this in *Towards a Theory of Drama in Education* (p 115).[4]

The timid child
This is the student who is apparently not participating. It is because he is too shy or too afraid to find his own way into the drama. The solution might be to:

- find ways to give him the opportunity to join: a simple question, the offering of a role, the assumption that he is participating.
- take the pressure off him by placing him so that he is not challenged by your eye contact. Be near or by him, but don't eye him!
- acknowledge but don't overpraise him when he does contribute.

The child who is unable to separate the real and the imagined world
Such students are often young or emotionally immature and continue in the role drama long after everyone else is out of role. Gently remind them that they are out of role and take particular care to allow time for debriefing and reflection.

The silent child
Such students are silent:

- because they don't know it is drama and that they can and are expected to contribute.
- because they are bored. This means that you have chosen something in which they do not perceive the challenge, or because you are over-using a strategy or technique.
- because they don't understand. This means that either the material is too complicated, or the 'play for the teacher' is overshadowing the 'play for them'.
- because they cannot see the logic of the development.
- because they are embarrassed, having been thrust into role without sufficient preparation or practice (this is particularly applicable to the older students):

- because the material is too close and full of connotations of reality, for example, playing a mother.
- because the material is remote from their experience so they do not know enough about it and they understand that drama should not be faked.
- because they see the teacher 'acting' or 'over-demonstrating' and they feel very awkward because there is no truth in it.
- because the teacher is a good role player, but, in an effort to stimulate, she is leaving no room for their contributions, and they take on the only role available, that of 'audience'.
- because they are tired. Role playing demands tremendous application and sometimes the timetable has exhausted them. You, as teacher, must recognize this and find another way of working. Note that the teacher is *never* tired, or rather, she never reveals her tiredness, unless, of course, she is in role and she chooses to add 'tired' to any of the general roles that we have listed.

Any of the above reasons apply equally to the individual or the group, but the silent individual within an active group may be very much involved and it is the teacher's responsibility to recognize this.

Pray that the above do not all appear in one class! These problems arise in other classes, but it is the immediacy of drama that brings them out. You should not see these influences as entirely negative. You can capitalize on these differences and use them to invigorate the work.

Grouping in role drama

Although it is advisable to begin a role drama with the group as a collective (for example, all are citizens of Thebes), there are many role groupings where points of view can vary or conflict. The teacher in role often represents the individual against or apart from the action, but her students need and should have this experience as well. Just as the teacher in role needs preparation, so do her students. The preparation may have to occur out of role (for example, reading about the gods) but often emerges from the dramatic exploration (for example, they can infer from the teacher, in role as Creon, the rules and power of the gods).

Examples of grouping

- The students in a whole group collective: for example, advisors to Creon
- Individual with another individual: Creon and his advisor
- Individual against an individual: Creon against Antigone
- Individual with the group: Antigone's nurse and the friends of Polynices
- Individual against the group: Creon against Antigone's friends
- Small group and large group: Creon's priests and the citizens of Thebes
- Small group against a large group: Antigone's supporters against the citizens of Thebes
- Half the group with the other half of the group: Antigone's friends appealing to the gods for help
- Half the group against the other half of the group: those who believe in the right decreed by the gods to bury the dead, against those who believe in adhering to Creon's law.

When working with half the group against half the group, each half should have had an opportunity to become familiar with the other's point of view before confronting each other. In this way the confrontation is a means of exploring the problem, rather than a forum for expressing an impasse!

> 'You're selfish!'
> 'No, we're not!'
> 'Yes, you are!'
> 'No, we're not!' . . .

General requirements for a teacher working in role

1 the ability to listen
2 the ability to pick up signals
3 flexibility
4 questioning skills
5 interest in how students learn
6 the courage to put herself at risk
7 the courage to fail, recognizing that failure is another way to success

8 the ability to conduct activities in an atmosphere of mutual respect
9 the pleasure in taking time to plan
10 the strength to be unthreatened by students' knowledge or suggestions
11 the courage to throw out her plan to go along with something the students suggest
12 the skill to slow down the action and not to rush the learning
13 the understanding to recognize when facts are or are not relevant
14 the knowledge of why she is using role playing.

Most teachers will already be exercising these skills and abilities in their teaching, so they should not be worried by undertaking a role. Role playing is the fastest way to find out whether your assumptions about your teaching are correct.

Things to consider before going into role

Before going into role the teacher must know how the role will contribute to learning. Having decided to use a role, what can the teacher do to support her own sense of role and help the students to accept her in it?

Knowledge

- know the period
- know the skills of the role (What can this person do?)
- know the attitude and point of view of the role
- know which of the above you will stress in order to enhance the learning objectives.

For example, if you take on the role of Lister,[5] how much do you know about:

- medicine in the 19th century?
- Lister's life and skills?
- how he felt and thought?
- his role as a researcher and a man of medicine?

Particularizing

Select from your knowledge the points you will use to enhance the role, particularizing a few details of your research to provide the focus for your students. For example, if you know that Lister recognized that cleanliness in the operating room saved lives but did not understand how germs spread disease: 'Gentlemen, in my operating room you will please wash your hands at the sink. Your cold is not much better, Dr Smith.'

Representing

Select those signals you will use to represent the role to your students:
Consider language: heightened and formalized for Lister.
Consider costume: sleeves rolled up.
Consider props: drying your hands on a towel (which is then handed on!)
Consider space: a formal set-up with a table.
Consider light: the table will be placed by the window.
As you and your students become more confident in working imaginatively, physical representation may become less necessary as they (and you) grow more capable of working symbolically.

Signalling

Just as every teacher learns to read her classes, so her students learn to read their teacher. When the teacher puts on her glasses they know that she means business. When she leans against her desk and folds her arms, they know the discussion will be informal. A quiet voice means trouble for the person addressed. *Signalling the attitudes and intentions* of the role clearly is the most important thing a drama teacher does when she is working in role.

Attitudes, points of view and intentions are created out of the teacher's knowledge and particularization of the role and are allied to the needs of her students (social and life skills) and the requirements of the curriculum. Voice, language, gesture and bearing which are appropriate to the drama, the role and the learning, must be carefully chosen and maintained. Knowing the background, what you are using and why you are using it make up the Substructure of your planning (see Chapter 6) and should never be abandoned if you see teacher in role as a fundamental technique to promote learning.

Warning!

Teachers who take up the challenge of working in role soon discover the pleasure of 'the play'. If you teach five classes of drama, try not to have more than one or two role dramas on the go at the same time. Even Peter Hall, Director of the National Theatre, finds directing three plays at once excessive!

Conclusion
In the theatre the director must eventually let go of the play and give it over to his actors. In role drama the more control and responsibility the teacher is able to hand over to her students, the more they are working, not only as 'performers' but as 'directors' and 'playwrights'. Teachers should be aware of the rich theatrical skill-building that her students will be engaged in as well as the wide cross-curriculum learning that is generated and fostered by their experiences in role drama.

A good play makes you think or feel. A great play makes you both think *and* feel. Good role drama makes you think or feel. Great role drama makes you both think *and* feel.

Skill building exercises for teachers
In numbers 1, 2 and 3 you will need to work with others.

1   To develop role perception
    Work in pairs.

    Task A: Look at the room you are in. On your own, note down anything in it that attracts your attention. Discuss with your partner the things you noted. If you noted different things, discuss why you may have done so. Has this anything to do with your 'personal luggage' of experiences?

    Task B: Look at the room through the eyes of an architect.
    In role, discuss with your partner the suitability of the space as a playroom for blind children. What changes and modifications would you both suggest?

Out of role, discuss the experience with your partner and note how it differs from the first task.

Task C: Look at the room through the eyes of a prisoner.
Talk to your partner in role.
Out of role, discuss the experience and how it differs from Tasks A and B.

You could choose other situations for practice. It is an interesting activity to do in different, less familiar environments, for example, with a friend on your way to work.

A question for discussion is: Are your other senses brought into action when you are in role?

Task D: Choose one of the three previous tasks or something new and see if you and your partner can move into dramatic action. It is sometimes useful to ask a third person to record what happens and to identify what prompted the action.

2   To develop signalling skills

Task A: Prepare and deliver an introductory role speech of one to two minutes, which tells who you are and who the listeners are, and sets out the problem or task to be tackled.
Suggestions:
(a) a policeman speaking to a group of recruits
(b) Claudius speaking to his court about Hamlet's behaviour
(c) a 'bag lady' (a happy transient who carries her worldly possessions around with her in carrier bags) talking to social workers.

Task B: Ask the listeners to list on the board words or phrases which describe the person they have met.

Task C: Go to the board.
Put a tick beside those things you wanted to signal.
Put an X beside those things you did not want or mean to signal.
Put an M beside those things that you know or feel are 'you'.
Put an A beside those things that are not 'you' but that you wanted them to see (A is for acting!)

Task D: If you have prepared one of (a), (b) or (c) above, could you say essentially the same thing but change the roles for the following?
(a) a guerilla leader speaking to a group of young rebels

(b) a prominent psychiatrist speaking to his colleagues on a case history

(c) a separatist speaking to federalists.

Does the language change? How? Why?
Does the meaning frame change, shift or remain the same?

3   To develop flexibility in the use of role (Groups of 5)

Task: One of you is 'teacher', the rest are the 'class'. A situation is given to the 'class' who initiate the action. The 'teacher' enters in a prescribed role and functions according to it. After each situation the 'class' identifies the role.

Here are some examples.

Situation	Role
(a) Prisoners planning an escape	Teacher as One of the Gang
(b) Pioneers just arrived in Canada from Europe, checking their papers and belongings	Teacher as Authority Outside the Action
(c) Archaeologists, having found a pot of great potential value, writing up their report	Teacher as Absentee
(d) A group of townspeople meeting to decide how to bring the old lodgekeeper down from Mount St Helens before it erupts	Teacher as Devil's Advocate
(e) A group of villagers at a well situated on land which has been purchased by a new vineyard owner	Teacher as Authority Opposed to the Group
(f) A group of trekkers crossing the veldt are confronted by a river in flood	Teacher as The Helpless
(g) A group of union workers on strike for better conditions	Teacher in the fringe role
(h) Reporters being briefed on making the news more 'appealing' to readers	Teacher as Authority
(i) The palace staff preparing for the return of the King and Queen after a civil uprising	Teacher as Second in Command

Questions for discussion:

- Could your 'class' identify your teaching role?
- Were you able to maintain it? If not, why not?
- How did you approach the group in the different roles?
- In which roles were you most comfortable? Why?
- Which roles promoted the most response from the 'class'?
- Which roles promoted the most learning? Why?

4 Rephrase the following into heightened language. For example: 'OK, so what are you going to look for?' to 'Let each man state the purpose of his quest.'

(a) Role: Second in Command
'Now kids, look hard and see how the good doctor soaks up the gore.'

(b) Role: Authority Outside the Action
'Boy! Some of you people sure don't know the rules!'

(c) Role: The Helpless
'Gee, King, sorry I was so stupid. I was just trying to help.'

(d) Role: The Absentee
'What's this about stepping up and giving the old "cross your heart and hope to die" bit?'

(e) Role: One of the Gang:
'Aw! Who cares! I'm tired of this whole thing!'

References
1 O'Neill, Cecily and Lambert, Alan, *Drama Structures*, p 13, Hutchinson, London, 1982
2 O'Neill, Cecily and Lambert, Alan, *Drama Structures*, p 63, Hutchinson, London 1982
3 Moffett, James, *The Universe of Discourse*
4 Bolton, Gavin, *Towards a Theory of Drama in Education*
5 Johnson and O'Neill, *Dorothy Heathcote: Collected Writing on Education and Drama*, pp 126–137, Hutchinson, London, 1984

_4_

Questioning and answering

Questioning

> Talking is the complementary experience to the sensory
> experience and enables the child to examine his
> experience with an awareness of its qualities.
> Joan Tough

> Questions draw language out of children (serving to lift)
> the level of thought in the learning process.
> Hilda Taba

> The question is central to learning.   Francis Hunkins

> Respecting the learner's autonomy, the teacher spends
> more time helping to articulate the urgent questions
> than demanding the right answers.   Marilyn Ferguson

When we were young and carefree, or rather, when we were at
school, we believed the good teacher knew everything about a
subject; she was a living textbook. If we listened hard and
answered her questions, we would become wise like her. If we
had any questions of our own they were mainly for clarification –
we hadn't understood what she had said or what she had asked
us to do. We were certain that we would be able to learn all there
was to know if we were so inclined and if we were prepared to
invest the time and energy.

In the past, children in school were expected to acquire
knowledge, and learning facts was an end in itself. For the
student today an effective memory is not the only requirement.
He must be able to react to what is being taught and must be

active in seeking understanding. In other words, he must seek, find and then be able to question what he has found in order to see all its facets, so that he may defend it or understand why it is no longer defensible. Knowledge is not only not finite, but the purveyors of knowledge can and must be questioned. 'Each student brings a different form of reference into the classroom, based on the sum of his knowledge, experience and values.'[1] The teacher's responsibility is five-fold:

- to discover what the student knows
- to discover what he understands
- to discover what he thinks and feels about his knowledge
- to discover what he needs to know
- to discover how to help him find that knowledge.

If the teacher ignores the affective aspect of the student's learning, she is denying him the opportunity of reaching the full potential of this learning. The process that the teacher constantly uses in weaving the fabric of learning is that of questioning. The teacher is never at any time breaking down what the student understands. She cannot because it is part of him. What she must do is present him with other ideas (implications, material, reasons) which will allow him to learn. For example (in a role drama):

Teacher: 'What shall we do with the injured Iroquois?'
Student: 'Kill him!'
The teacher may say: 'Do you think that is necessary?'
Function: looking for reasons

or
Teacher: 'How shall we find our way to the river then?'
Function: suggesting implications

or
Teacher: 'I found this ring on his finger. Is it not of European design?'
Function: to introduce new material.

If the killing has already taken place it is a *fait accompli*. To say 'Thou shalt not kill' or 'Oh dear, we shouldn't have done that' is useless. In drama the teacher must deal with what is given:

Teacher: 'What shall we do with the body?'
Function: to introduce new material: every killing leaves a body.

or

Teacher: 'How will they seek their revenge? Does anyone
            know how a scalp is taken?'
Function: to deal with implications and to offer the possibility
            of a short research project which will satisfy their
            desire for blood!

The reflection which either of these questions generates, gives
the students an opportunity for further thought and research.
'Did we really need to kill him?' and, perhaps, 'I wonder what
drives someone to take another person's life?'. These doors for
new learning, when opened by the teacher, can lead to a shift
in understanding.[2]

General teaching skills in questioning

The following general teaching skills need to be emphasized in
a book such as this.

- The teacher is responsible for the arrangement of the space
  and her place in that space (whether still or on the move).
- She ensures that all the students are in a position to see and
  hear during discussion, so that all may be involved.
- She makes and maintains eye contact.
- She listens seriously, giving consideration to all answers.
- She uses her voice to create and support interest.
- She is responsible for the establishment of the ritual of
  permission to answer. This may be formal, where everything
  comes through the teacher, either by raising a hand, taking
  turns, standing up, or passing the 'talking stick'. Alternatively, it may be informal, so that, in a free-flow conversation,
  the teacher is simply a contributing member of the group.
  However, she still has the responsibility of maintaining the
  focus and encouraging the development of the discussion.
- She ensures that all who have something to say are encour-
  aged to contribute.
- She ensures that in any one-on-one dialogue, she includes
  the whole group through eye contact, and finds opportunities
  to throw the subject open to the group.

If all the above are in place, an easy atmosphere should prevail
where there is a general respect for the ideas and opinions of all.
    Although questioning would seem to fall under general

teacher training, it is the *way* in which questioning is conducted in drama which must be investigated and practised. In much of everyday teaching, the teacher is dealing with material for which she knows the answers. The questions are therefore asked so as to reveal whether the students know the answer that the teacher knows. In drama, the teacher, as Dorothy Heathcote says, is 'seldom in the stance of one who knows'. She is most often asking the question precisely because she does not know the answer and is dependent upon the student's answer in order to move the drama on.

Questioning in drama presents two problems:

1   How to phrase the question in order to tap into the student's knowledge, understanding and experience.
2   How to handle the answer. Questioning in drama is almost always cumulative and the teacher must have the ability to weave the answers into the dramatic context.

In structuring a drama lesson or unit, a good teacher will have a number of prepared questions ready through which she ascertains whether the students know the required facts, for example, 'Do you know what a farrier is?', or at what level the students are prepared to work, for example, 'Would you like to find out what a farrier is, or do you want me to tell you?' But it is the questions that occur *within* the drama, through role or reflection (in or out of role), which often appear to be the most difficult to frame. In other words, the teacher cannot prepare for them as they occur in context, and their wording is suggested by the situation and/or the role. It is this high-risk situation, working in the moment without a net, that can inhibit a drama teacher, denying herself and her students a deeper and more satisfying learning experience. Unless the teacher infuses the questions with an expression of genuine curiosity and a real desire to hear the answer, she will find herself faced with shallow thinking, revealed in trite answers which waste everyone's time.

The characteristics of a drama question

- It is the expressive demonstration of a genuine curiosity.
- It occurs in context and relates to the experience.
- The words are ordered in such a way as to support the role and clarify the thinking. For example, in a drama where the success of the journey is dependent upon the horses, to ask

'What kind of horses do you have?' invites the answer, 'Two black ones and a Palamino', which has nothing to do with the essence of horse in the situation. It would be better to ask: 'Looking at the horses you have chosen, can you reassure us that they will be able to withstand the hardships of the journey ahead?' This question gives information (it will probably be a hard journey), shows that the farrier has a responsibility to the horses and to the group who are all dependent on the horses, and sets up a dramatic possibility (something might happen to the horses).

- The intent of the question must be supported by intonation and non-verbal signals on the part of the questioner.
- The pace of the question must relate to the situation. For example, if the enemy is close at hand, the question 'Are we ready to leave?' must be expressed with an urgency quite different from that of the leisurely planning of an orderly departure.

Most important of all:

- The teacher must know why she is asking the question; it should have reason, focus and curiosity.
- She should remember that 'in Drama there is no right answer. The teacher is not asking questions to which there is a single appropriate response.'[3]

Kinds of questions

We have used *Rumplestiltskin* as the source of all questions in Sections A, B and C. Our Dramatic Focus is: keeping a promise.

A *Questions which concretize the outer discipline of the work: rules, form, content, plot and action*

1 Establishing the rules of the game

These questions generally begin with the phrase 'are we all agreed', 'do we all agree that', summarizing the information and decisions which have come from the group.

Example: 'Are we all agreed that we are in the service of the Queen?'

Function: These agreements with the class allow the teacher to remind students, if necessary, of *their* rules of play.

2   Assessing student interest
Example: 'Would you like to find out what happens next?'
Function: to catch the students in the net of the lesson which is developing.

3   Seeking information
Example: 'Where will we meet the Queen?'
Function: to establish location and assess the expectations of the class. If the students reply 'a council room', then it is apparent that they expect a meeting which will be formal and ritualistic. If they reply 'in the barn', then their expectation is of intrigue and secrecy. In either case, the teacher can structure accordingly.

4   Asking for facts
Example: 'In those days, what would the guard be carrying to protect the Queen?'
Function: to establish an historical understanding in order to avoid anachronisms which might cause difficulties such as TV/ lasers/bazookas appearing at inconvenient moments!

5   Requiring the student to think beyond the initial response
Example: 'What exactly do you mean by "in the barn"?'
Function: to get the student to clarify what he has said for himself, others and the teacher, so that they all know they are talking about the same thing.

Example: 'Why do you think the barn is a good place?'
Function: to prompt the student to defend his answer.

Example: 'If we go to the barn, what difficulties/advantages might there be?'
Function: to force the students to look at the implications of their suggestion.

Example: 'John, you've been very quiet, what do you think of this suggestion?'
Function: to redirect the question so as to allow others to enter the discussion, rather than simply assenting to the idea.

6 Defining the moment

Example: 'At what time of the day would the Queen want to meet us?'

Function: to clarify time and to let the teacher into the students' ideas; it also establishes hierarchy: we are at the Queen's command.

7 Stimulating research/task

Example: 'Where could we find a picture that would show us how far the barn is from the castle?'; 'Could we draw a plan of the castle grounds?'

Function: to encourage the students to plan, to slow down the action, and to generate some dramatic possibilities for the children.

8 Unifying

Example: 'Are we all agreed that the Queen's secret must be kept?'

Function: to ensure that we all have the same action focus.

9 Supplying information

Example: 'What excuse will you use if you are challenged by the guards of the nightwatch as you make your way through the castle grounds to the great barn?'

Function: to prepare the students to deal with a possible challenge; to imply that people don't wander around at night; and to remind them that the castle is defended and so add the Tension that things may go wrong.

Example: 'What was the password we agreed upon?'

Function: to give the students responsibility for recollecting information.

Example: 'With all the difficulties we might encounter, is there someone who can review the plans for us so that we are all clear?'

Function: to give the students responsibility for sequencing the information.

Example: 'Did you know that each guard carries only his halberd?'

Function: to supply simple information; if the students disagree and say that he is armed to the teeth, the teacher is prepared.

Example: 'How do we know that Rumplestiltskin won't put a spell on us?'
Function: to slow down (if not stop dead!) the action by recalling information from which a logical inference is made through the question.

10   Helping establish or control group discipline
Example: 'How do we talk to the Queen without being overheard?'
Function: to keep the noise level down.

Example: 'How shall we organize the order in which we leave the castle?'
Function: to control movement.

Example: 'How should we greet the Queen in these secret circumstances?'
Function: to establish the ritual, which by its nature is a control (see Chapter 5, page 131, Ritual).

11   Offering choice
Note that you should not offer a choice unless you are prepared to accept the student's selection!

Example: (a) 'Do you want to talk to the King, or do you want to talk to Rumplestiltskin?'
Function: a simple choice of either/or, the choice is absolutely unweighted. (Note that a student may offer a third choice, 'It's her secret. I think we should ask the Queen first').

Example: (b) The same question phrased slightly differently, but still a choice question: 'Do you want to tell the King, or interview Rumplestiltskin?'
Function: to dictate the form the drama will take. The students will either have to plan the questions they are going to ask Rumplestiltskin, or decide how and how much they will tell the King.

Example: (c) 'Do you want to tell the King about the bargain or do you want to persuade Rumplestiltskin to give up his claim to the baby?'
Function: to dictate the content of the telling and the persuading.

Note that in all the questions the teacher has limited the choice, but in (c), where both form and content are suggested, the play is now more the teacher's than the students'.

Often in an either/or question, the students will decide to compromise, keeping both doors open: 'Let's talk to Rumplestiltskin first, then we'll know what to say to the King.' or 'Let's talk to Rumplestiltskin first and then we may not need to talk to the King.'

When working with very young students, Davies[4] suggests that presenting the children with clear alternatives is a good way to encourage them to begin decision-making in drama and unifies their foci. He offers these choices:

Topic: 'Shall we go to the Queen or ask her to come to us?'
Role: 'Shall we be the Queen's Royal Advisors or her friends?'
Place: 'Shall we meet in the barn or in the castle?'
Time: 'Shall we meet during the day or at night?'
Attitude: 'Do we want to believe that the Queen has done her best or do we think that she has behaved badly?'
Direction: 'Would we like Rumplestiltskin to appear at this meeting or do we want to talk to the Queen alone first?'

B   Questions which help to shape the inner understanding

1   Building identification
Examples: 'How long have you been in the service of the Queen?'
          'How will you leave your quarters without your family or servants hearing you?'
Function: to build autobiography through teacher-assisted elaboration of role.

Example: 'Do you all have a dark garment to cover yourselves?'
Function: to help the student visualize himself in the drama.

2   Establishing commitment
Example: 'How can we prove to the Queen that we are loyal?'
Function: to have students suggest a binding ritual, such as the swearing/signing of an oath, which can be used later as a

negotiation point: 'When you signed, did you know it was going to be this difficult?'

Example: 'How many of you are prepared to put your thumbprint to this oath?'
Function: to require an overt demonstration of commitment, not only to the drama but to the lesson itself. (You must be prepared for some to refuse).

Example: 'Will you now begin to make your preparations for this night's business?'
Function: through task, the teacher allows the students time to build their own demonstration of readiness, often accompanied by narration or voice-over (see Chapter 5, page 142, Narration).

3 Helping to deepen insight into the problem: inference and interpretation
Example: 'Did Rumplestiltskin want the Queen's baby from the very beginning?'
Function: to question motives.

Example: 'Surely the Miller's daughter could have promised something else?'
Function: to give the students the experience of trying to find an alternative. They are facing the same problem that the miller's daughter faced.

Example: 'What will happen to us if our King dies and we have given the heir away to a stranger?'
Function: to imply that the baby has an importance beyond the immediate concern of its mother.

Example: 'In order to save her life, the Queen made a promise, how *can* she keep that promise?'
Function: to face the students with the fact that promises must be kept.

Example: 'Can you buy friendship and love, or must you earn them?'
Function: to focus on the future relationship of Rumplestiltskin and the baby.

4 Establishing relationships
Example: (To students in role) 'You have children, could you imagine what it would be like to give up your eldest child?'

Function: to ask for a personal response through role, relating to the student's family ties and his perception of his role in his own family.

Example: 'Does anyone know the story of Solomon?'
Function: to relate the same problem to another story and time.

Example: 'I wonder if there are times when we are justified in breaking our promises?'
Function: to relate to the student's own life. (This kind of question should be rhetorical, that is to say, the teacher is merely hoping to promote thought.)

C Questions that 'press' the students to 'a deeper consideration of the situation'[5]

Unlike the earlier questions, which call for elaboration in order to clarify the students' ideas, these questions are based on the teacher's learning focus (the 'play for the teacher'). They only occur in role when the students have the confidence to withstand the pressure.

1 Challenging

Some fine examples of the 'press' were used out of role by Dorothy Heathcote when she was teaching in Vancouver in 1983. To some children who were prepared to solve the problem of contaminated water in their hospital by bringing in water planes from Seattle, she said: 'Do you want the easy solution, or do you want to make it real?' On another occasion in the same drama, she took the children out of role to say, 'That's the answer children would give. I thought we were working as adults here.' Although some of the teachers watching were very concerned at Heathcote's abrupt confrontation with her students, the children accepted these challenges without offence and leapt back into the work with vigour and creative energy.

The following questions in role become more challenging as they progress:
'I understand why you want to tell the King, but did we not all sign the oath of secrecy?'
Function: to remind students of their previous commitment.

'Are you, each one of you, prepared to ignore the oath sworn by all of us?'

Function: a stronger reminder of the learning focus – promises must be kept. Note the heightened language and the repetition. (The tone is full of implication.)
'What then, shall I do with this?' (Teacher holds up the oath of secrecy which they have all signed.)
Function: the teacher's words and action serve as a direct challenge to the students.

If the students' response to this challenge is still soft, the teacher must recognize that her focus for the drama is not operating. (See Chapter 6, page 171, Dramatic Focus.)

2   Asking for a 'feeling' response

While knowing can be divorced from feeling, understanding has affective connotations. Drama teachers are often accused of prying into students' feelings. 'How do you feel?' is one way to identify a drama teacher! Teachers need to know which methods of questioning will encourage students to express answers at the feeling level without exposing them to the risk of becoming embarrassed or being laughed at. Heathcote suggests that asking questions directed at the student's *concerns* will elicit answers invested with feeling, but which appear 'cooler' in expression and offer a much richer 'soil' for forwarding the drama.

Questions that ask a student 'How do you feel?' or 'How do you feel now that the King's guard knows that we are here?', can often produce a superficial or dismissive answer, such as 'I feel frightened' or 'I feel angry'. These answers may reflect real meaning or merely be giving the reply the teacher is indicating that she expects through her tone and non-verbal signals. For this sort of reply to be of any use, the teacher must press with another question such as 'How frightened are you?' or 'Why are you angry?'. This probing on the part of the teacher as an extension to a 'feeling' question is often misconstrued by the student as 'prying' at a personal rather than a role level. A student's feelings are his to reveal or not as he wishes. The drama teacher must not pry into the student's private world and her questions must allow the student to give freely or not at all. Rephrasing the question as 'What is your concern now that the King's guard knows that we are here?' and receiving the answer 'Somebody told on us' gives the teacher an insight into the student's feeling of betrayal and/or loss of purpose (and also provides her with another route, allied to the focus of keeping promises, in the identification of the traitor).

To recapitulate: feelings need a context for expression. In

answering appropriate questions, the students are required to reflect, thus supplying both the context and opportunities for expressing feelings.

Example: 'Were you, at any time, afraid/concerned/worried?'
Function: to slow down the action by requiring the student to give what has occurred order and significance.

Examples: 'What is your concern at the moment?'
                    'What is on your mind?'
                    'What are you thinking about at this moment?'
Function: to slow down the action; although the student is thinking in the present, his concern will be expressed either in reflection (what has happened) or projection (what will happen).

Example: 'What would you tell your grandchildren about this experience?'
Function: as above, but also demanding the ability to select the most significant points and to give them expression.

None of the above questions are guaranteed to produce expressions of feeling, but they have the potential to reveal feeling without it being seen as prying by the teacher.

3   Requiring value judgements
This kind of question can occur at any time in the making of the drama or as part of the reflective activities.

Examples: 'Do you think we *are* right to keep the secret from the king?'
                    'Was it honest of us to hold a secret meeting and deceive our families?'
Function: the students are required to make their *own* value judgements. The teacher's values will have prompted the question!

Other questions that are useful: 'Was it/is it considerate/wise/foolish/good/bad/wrong/dishonest?'

4   Developing supposition and/or critical assessment
Example: 'What do you think would have happened/would happen if Rumplestiltskin and the Queen had taken their problem to the King?'
Function: to give the students the opportunity to finish the story in a different way. It is important for them to recognize

that there is an alternative and that other ways of solving problems can be found through discussion or through action (acting out).

Other phrases which are useful:

'What could we have done differently?'
'What if we had done/hadn't done . . .?'
'Have you thought what might happen if . . .?'
'Can you imagine what . . .?'
'I wonder what would have happened/would happen if . . .?'
'What would it be like if? . . .'

One of the most exciting things we can do in drama is to explore 'the road not taken'. Can you imagine what sort of play there might have been if Antigone had not buried her brother but obeyed Creon's command?

D   Other kinds of questions

1   Closed questions
These are questions with 'Yes' or 'No' answers.

In drama where the intent is to develop the student's thinking, decision-making and verbal skills, closed questions are not generally regarded as productive. However they do have some uses.

- As a check: 'Are you ready to go?'
- As a summary: 'Then we all know the procedure for tonight?'
- As a review: 'Is it agreed that we wait until the lights go out and the clock in the tower strikes two before we leave?'
- To move on: 'Then we don't need to practise our bows?'

2   Questions that summarize
Example: 'Can someone tell us the procedure for tonight's business?'
Function: the students have the responsibility for recapitulating the plan.

3   Clarifying for the teacher
Examples: 'Am I right in thinking . . .?'
                   'Do I understand you to mean . . .?'

'What you are saying is . . .?'
'Do you mean that . . .?'
Function: the teacher is seen to be thinking aloud, sorting out
the replies, ideas and comments of the students who know that
they can interrupt to correct if she is wrong.

4   Building tension
Example: 'How high does the tide come?'
Function: to offer a moment of tension which the students may
accept or reject. 'It only comes to here' (indicating knees) offers
a safe way out, while 'Here is the tide line' (indicating above his
head) suggests a desire for a predicament.

Example: 'Stop a moment! Did anyone hear anything?'
Function: as above, but with the added *frisson* that if they accept
that something has been heard, they don't know whether it will
be good or bad.

Example: 'How many more people in the group have these
marks?'
Function: as above, but the students may be required to demonstrate if they are marked or unmarked, thus introducing the
possibility of a split in the group.

Example: 'I wonder if they have started looking for us yet?'
Function: to reinforce the cohesion of the group and, at the
same time, deny them the opportunity of avoiding the tension.

5   The question as the 'lure'
Often a seemingly innocuous question can be made to operate
as a lure because the tone opposes the meaning. This effect is
dependent upon what has gone before in the drama and the
tension, or lack of it, in the situation. Cecily O'Neill, working
with students who were doing a play about being left on a desert
island, approached a group on the 'beach' and told them that it
was no use their expecting to be picked up by the tour boat, as
the tides would not permit this. She assured them that the boat
would return in the morning, and asked if they would like to
spend the night at her house. At her 'house' she offered them
something to drink in the kindest way possible (quite a few
refused though none could tell why) and then said to the group
who were looking around: 'I see you are interested in my sculp-
tures. They *are* very lifelike, aren't they?' An icy chill was
apparent immediately!

   The lure is a means of (a) getting the students (in role) into the power of the teacher (in role) or (b) throwing the students off balance in what was previously a comfortable and rather ordinary situation.

6   Offering an opportunity to rethink or restate
Examples: 'You still think that?'
                  'You've changed your mind?'
Function: to give the student an opportunity to reconsider his original response.

Example: 'What made you change your mind?'
Function: to give the student an opportunity of elaborating on the generally short responses expected from questions and of testing out his new view of a situation.

Some other considerations in questioning

1   Intonation
The teacher can use her tone of voice or a change of pace to make any question a threat or challenge.
Example: 'Is that all the grain collected today?'
Function: (a) as a clarifier, meaning 'is there more to come?'
                  (b) as a concern, meaning 'it will be a hard winter'
                  (c) as a threat, meaning 'you had better improve on that'
                  (d) as a challenge, meaning 'you are incapable of working hard'.

2   Non-verbal questions
Teachers should be aware of the power of:

* raising an eyebrow ('Why would you want to do that?')
* shrugging the shoulders ('Who cares?', 'Is that important?')
* opening the palms upwards ('What shall we do?')
* the silence in which the teacher looks at the group ('Do you all agree with that?')

3   Minimal encouragements
Example: 'Mm . . . hmmmm.'
Function: to indicate that the teacher is interested in what is

being said. It is a prompt that indicates to the student that he is to continue.

The repetition of one or two key words constitutes another kind of minimal encouragement. Other examples are: 'Oh . . .', 'So . . .', 'Then . . .', 'Ummmm . . .', 'Hmmmm . . .', 'Uhhuh . . .', 'Right . . .', 'Go on . . .'. Gavin Bolton uses this technique to great advantage in his work with students.

4 The use of 'Why?'
'Why?' has so often been misused that its original meaning has become distorted. It now tends to suggest disapproval or displeasure, and can invite defensiveness, withdrawal, or conversely, attack. It is often difficult for a student to know 'why' and there may be several possibilities. 'Why?' questions can be used to obtain factual information, but should be avoided on personal levels.[6]

Summary

Questions are first and foremost an opportunity for clarifying and testing out meaning and understanding for both the teacher and for her students. The usual understanding is that it is in the answers that this happens but it is important to recognize that the making of a question serves the same function and is of equal importance. The great strength of drama as a medium of learning is that it is an area in which both teacher and students are working together in the imaginative context. Questions are not the sole prerogative of the teacher and answers are not only for students.

Situations which promote student questioning

The interview

Here one student interviews another, or the group interviews a student, or the student interviews the group. The function of the interviewer is to draw out information appropriate to the task or role. The function for the interviewee is to provide (or conceal) the information, which action may help to clarify his thinking.

The investigation
Here one or more students are involved in a discovery, formulating and asking questions which build facts into a logical whole, for example, detectives, anthropologists.

The trial
Here the students not only ask questions but must anticipate questions which may be asked.

Market research
Here the students must particularize and focus the kinds of questions to use.

Drama roles which promote student questioning

The Learner
The student wants to know. The responsibility for guiding is on the responder.

The Absentee
The student is filling in the gaps; he has a framework within which to question.

The Researcher
The student focuses strongly on a particular area; he wants to find out.

The Interviewer
The student is building a general understanding; his focus is on the person being interviewed.

The Media Reporter
The student is finding an opinion; the focus is external to both interviewer and interviewee.

The Policeman
The student is looking for facts; the focus is on what is or was.

The Detective
The student is looking for clues; his questions are designed to be indirect, divergent.

The Interrogator
The student is discovering a truth, whatever this may be.

The Lawyer
The student is building a case; the focus is on protecting his client.

The Devil's Advocate
The student is taking one side in order to promote the other; the focus is to challenge.

The Inquisitor
The student is extorting a confession; he knows what he wants to hear, but questions are indirect; like the detective, he is looking for incongruencies.

Using concrete objects to stimulate questions

When examining concrete objects, the students are required to hypothesize and develop a logical and satisfactory story by questioning not only the object, but each other. In this way they clarify, qualify and test out other people's reasoning and defend their own. O'Neill and Lambert begin 'The Way West'[7] by presenting the class with an old photograph of a group of pioneers standing by their wagons. Well chosen artifacts may also serve as a stimulus for explorations in drama work. The use of an outsider with a story to be drawn out by the students, is also an effective means of generating questions from the students (Stranger in Role). Other examples of concrete objects which can be used in this way are drawings (done by another class), a time capsule, letters and the teacher's own collection of objects.

Often the students' own work (letters written in role, for example) or their own belongings can serve. A class who had begun with an imaginative exercise in tight-rope walking, moved into a drama about refugees crossing into a free country. Before leaving for the final dash, the teacher, in role, asked them to give up anything they had that might identify them and to write a short letter which would be sent to their next of kin if they were not successful. After they had set out, the drama was moved forward twenty years. The students changed into the roles of investigators examining a cache which had been found near the mountains. By examining their own possessions and letters they built up the story of what had happened to the refugees.

When introducing a person, picture or object, the teacher may choose to know everything, something, little or nothing, depending on the kind of questioning processes she wishes her students to undertake.

Answering

> The responses of the class will demonstrate a great deal about the level of thinking in the group.[8]

In tennis, the server is not only concerned with the quality of her service, but must also be prepared for the return. Similarly, the questioner must not be satisfied with asking challenging questions but must know how to deal with the answers in order to promote a dialogue giving satisfaction to both questioner and answerer.

General teaching skills

- The teacher must feel comfortable with silence. She must be prepared to give the students time to think.
- She must be prepared to wait for the answer, reinforcing the fact that she is looking for something more than the easy answer.
- She must be able to listen to the answer with interest.
- She must acknowledge the answer, either non-verbally, by comment or by further questioning.
- She must ensure that everyone has heard the answer.

However, she will not repeat every answer as this encourages the students to listen only to her.
- She must be prepared to repeat or reword her question if the students are having difficulty.
- She must be alert to pick up the *sotto voce* answers in an informal discussion.
- She must be alert to the unvoiced answer – the reaction of the group.
- She must avoid collecting answers until she gets the one she wants.
- She must be able to distinguish between the 'smart-alec' answer and the genuine answer based upon a misunderstanding.

Special skills in handling responses

The following examples are drawn from a lesson on the movement of the United Empire Loyalists from Upper New York State to the Niagara Peninsula (Fort Niagara), Canada.

Situation: The students, in role as loyalists, have found and taken prisoner an Iroquois scout.
Teacher: 'What shall we do about him?'
Students: 'Kill him!'
The teacher has put herself at considerable risk in asking this question as she recognizes the answer is a valid solution, though not the one with which she is comfortable.

Response repertoire
1   Ignore the answer and wait.
    She accepts by her silence, but is hoping that someone will suggest something else.
2   'Ye..e..es.'
    She acknowledges verbally that she has heard the answer but, as above, is waiting for another idea.
3   'How?'
    This question does not move the drama in any direction or supply anything other than an invitation to reproduce the latest violence from the silver screen.
4   'Yes. That is a way to handle the situation.'
    She has accepted but left room for other suggestions.
5   'Yes. That is one way we could handle the situation.'

This suggests that there are other ways that could be investigated.

6   'Yes. You feel he is a danger to us if we let him live?'
    She has accepted the idea of killing, but is demanding that the students justify their solution.

7   'Yes. We could put him out of action.'
    Through euphemism, she is implying that there are ways other than killing to accomplish the same end.

8   'If we kill him, won't his tribe seek revenge?'
    She is suggesting cause and effect implications.

9   'Do we want to be savages too?'
    At first glance this question has a certain dramatic challenge to it. But unless the teacher wishes to focus the students on to an examination of fallacy (if we kill we are savages: *ergo* all savages kill), she should avoid it.

10 'Yes, but then we may never know the secrets of the forest.'
    Here the teacher accepts the solution but regrets the implications of it. This should allow the students an opportunity to rethink.

The teacher can respond to the idea of killing with any of the above. She may choose to start with number 10 and move back until she finds an appropriate response to generate reflection.

Questions 1, 2 and 3 simply postpone the inevitable.

Questions 4, 5, 6 and 7 open the way to other ideas.

Question 8 helps the students to look at implications.

Question 10 invites the students into a discussion of values.

Drawing out answers

Teacher: 'What shall we do now?'

Students: (No answer)

The following actions are now possible.

1   Teacher waits.
    Function: to suggest that there is more to come and that there is an answer.

2   Teacher rephrases: 'Shouldn't we do something?'
    Function: to clarify the teacher's meaning, making it more accessible to the students ('We need to take action').

3   Teacher: 'Mary, you've scouted ahead and seen the river, what do you advise?'
    Function: to direct the question at an individual whose expertise can be relied upon.

4 Teacher: 'Didn't I hear someone mention a boat?'
    Function: to plant a seed which might lead to 'growth'.
5 Teacher: 'Are you prepared to go on watch if we remain?'
    Function: to press.
6 Teacher: 'I'm not staying here. Who will come with me?'
    Function: to challenge.

Upgrading thought and language

Thought
In listening to the answers and responding to them, the teacher
has an opportunity to fit them into the context, making individual
answers relevant to the whole group and indicating through
elaboration the implications of the responses.

Teacher: 'What will we need in the fort?'
Student: 'Guns.'
Teacher: 'Yes. We may have to defend ourselves.'
Function: to accept, but also to offer an insight into the group's
            in-role vulnerability.
Student: 'We'll need food.'
Teacher: (Nodding) 'We may have to stay here a long time.'
Function: to offer implications.

Language
Teacher in role: 'What is your report of the battle?'
Student in role: 'We creamed 'em.'
Teacher in role: 'Yes. Our superiority is obvious.'
Function: to bring the language into the context of the drama.

Teacher out of role: 'What do we want to happen in this battle?'
Student out of role: 'We'll cream 'em.'
Teacher out of role: 'Ah! In what ways will we be superior?'

In role drama, the teacher can model language for her
students and this subtle upgrading is a safe way of correcting
which the students accept without taking personal offence.
However, upgrading and rephrasing everything the students say
is as misdirected as repeating their answers, so do not use it too
often.

Dealing with a response which downgrades another's contribution

Student: 'Aw! That's stupid!'

Teacher: 'So far, it's the only idea we have.'
Function: to give acknowledgement to the contribution, implying that others should try contributing.

Teacher: 'Perhaps, but do you have a better idea?'
Function: to remind students of the rules of brainstorming.

Teacher: 'Hold it! We're just brainstorming here!'
Function: a more overt reminder of brainstorming.

Teacher: 'Just a moment! Do we really understand what he said?'
Function: to show the student who has made what was considered a stupid remark that the teacher is prepared to consider it.

Teacher: 'Out of role for a moment. Is that the way a soldier would speak to his captain?'
Function: to go out of role so that the student can face the implications of his role.

Teacher: 'I am prepared to listen to all ideas.'
Function: to encourage the students to put forward more ideas.

If the remark is truly stupid it will be due to thoughtlessness, inattention, or the desire to disrupt, and should be dealt with accordingly. We generally do it with a look, or 'I think he forgot where he was', or 'Doesn't seem to make sense, does it?' and *move on*.

Analyzing the answer

The answer can be analyzed for what is relevant and irrelevant, and for what may be useful later.

Teacher: 'Where did you find the scout?'
Student: 'We found him in the ditch beside the road, with his head bashed in.'

What is relevant: The Indian was alone or abandoned when found.

What is irrelevant: the 'road'. Roads did not exist in the forest through which these people were travelling in the late eighteenth century. However, the anachronism is irrelevant to the situation at that moment. If the teacher is working for historical accuracy she may rephrase 'beside the road' to 'beside the trail' and continue.

What is on hold: Who bashed his head in? One of his own people? If so, why? Could he have been trying to make contact with us? Are there other enemies? Might they be our friends? Have we become involved in some sort of tribal war?

Teacher's response: 'Did you search the woods for signs of other people?'

Function: to clarify what is relevant.

Giving an answer weight

In the sharing of information about the site where the scout was found, the teacher hears someone say, 'Just looked like the same old forest to me.' Although this response sounds rather casual, the teacher may choose to give it weight by saying: 'Looked as it has always looked? Could someone have successfully covered their traces. We know they are clever at this?' This rephrasing and slight upgrading of language takes up the line of the student's thinking, even if he said it unthinkingly, and begins to probe gently into the dramatic possibilities of 'what is on hold'.

Universalizing the answer

Student 1 in role   'Are we ready to move off?'

Student 2 in role: 'We'll stay behind to cover the tracks.'

Teacher in role: 'There always have to be people who risk their lives in order for progress to be assured.'

Function: using the power of the universal to strengthen the responsibility of the students to their roles and the action they have chosen. They are a part of that group of people who clean up after nuclear accidents; work in a leper colony; look for a cure for AIDS.

Reasons why students don't answer questions

- The answer is too obvious.
- They are shy.
- They are afraid of answering incorrectly.
- They are naturally taciturn.
- They think the teacher is prying into their personal lives.
- They are afraid of embarrassing themselves in front of their peers.
- Answering questions may not be 'cool'.

- Or perhaps they are silent because they are thinking.

The teacher's own silence can often be used as a subtle pressure which says in effect, 'I have asked a question. I am prepared to wait because I know that you need time to think seriously about your answer.' A good teacher, as we have said before, is comfortable with a 'thinking' silence, her own and her students'.

Analysis of questions used in a drama lesson

The following is an account of a drama lesson with 20 five-year-olds, using a picture book story as source. Column 1 numbers the questions for your reference. Columns 2 and 3 show the Level of Personal Engagement and the Category of Identification. This is not a complete account of the lesson, nor is it a perfect lesson, but it does show how questions from teacher and students can promote understanding at both the plot and the feeling level.

Conclusion
A good answer depends upon the care with which the question is put. It is not just framing the question that is important. The teacher should know what kind of thinking and what level of feeling engagement she is trying to generate in the response. However, in the final analysis, we would rather have a class full of unanswered questions than one full of unquestioned answers!

> The open teacher . . . establishes rapport and resonance, sensing unspoken needs, conflicts, hopes, and fears. Respecting the learner's autonomy, the teacher spends more time helping to articulate the urgent questions than demanding right answers.[9]

Source: *The Three Poor Tailors*, by V. G. Ambrus[10]
Grade: Kindergarten
Time: 1½ hours with a short break

Who asks	Description	Question number	Level of Personal Engagement	Category of Identification	Notes
Teacher:	Teacher reads title and shows the children the book and the picture of the tailors at work making an important-looking coat. 'What does a tailor do?'	1	1		To establish that tailoring is a profession and to ensure that the children do not confuse a tailor with Mr and Mrs Taylor who live next door.
Teacher:	'Can you show me?'	2	2		
	Teacher adopts a fringe role (see page 48). She asks individual children.				
Teacher:	'What are you making?'	3	2	1	To test agreement. To 'accept the Big Lie'.
Child A:	'A coat for the mayor.'				
Teacher:	'Why did he choose that colour?'	4	2		
	Teacher reads the story to the point where 'they were always so busy that not one of them had been there (the city).'				
Teacher:	'I wonder what the big city is like?'	5	2		
Teacher:	'I wonder whether we could go to the city?'	6	2		
	Enthusiastic response			1	

Who asks	Description	Question number	Level of Personal Engagement	Category of Identification	Notes
Teacher:	'What kinds of building would we see?'	7	2		Teacher finds out the kind of city the children are anticipating.
	The children described 'their' city which included: MacDonald's, a big department store, tall buildings, library, no trees, hotels. They then drew pictures on the wall at one end of the room.				
Teacher:	'How shall we get to the city?'	8	1	1	
Children:	'Bus, car, train.'				
Teacher:	'Shall we see how the other tailors travelled?'	9	2	1	Teacher is reengaging the children.
	The tailors travelled by nanny goat and the children decided they would travel by horse, donkey or goat (four-footed animals), one per person.				
Teacher:	'What shall we need in the big city?'	10	2	1	Children work from experience or from projection.
	Group decided they needed 'money and something to put the money in to keep it safe'.				
Teacher:	'How much money shall we take?	11	1	1	A badly worded question as the children's answers varied from 25c to a billion dollars.
Teacher:	Rewords. 'What might we need money for?'	12	2		Rewording to recoup.

Who asks	Description	Question number	Level of Personal Engagement	Category of Identification	Notes
Children:	'Food, things in shops, movies.'				
Child A:	'Some cloth.'			3	This child is 'thinking tailor'.
Teacher:	Much discussion ensued (a mini maths lesson) then the children settled for $10 per person.				Opportunity here for a maths lesson. The teacher was restricted in time as it was a demonstration lesson.
Teacher:	'Shall we have it in one big purse or shall we be responsible for our own?'	13	3		
Children:	Answers varied from 'We might lose it' (shouted down), 'We might get lost', 'We might want to do different things'. It was decided that they would keep their own and carry it in a safe place.			1 (for most)	
	The children prepared for the journey with their money in a safe place. Horses were harnessed. The tailor shop was locked.				Ritual of departure for a journey (see page 131)
Child B:	'What if someone wants some new clothes while we are away?'	14	4	3	
	The children decided to leave a note on the door.				
Teacher:	'What shall we put on the note?'	15	5		Child anticipates the question the teacher had planned to ask.

Who asks	Description	Question Number	Level of Personal Engagement	Category of Identification	Notes
	Further discussion, then the children decided: *Closed* *will open Wednesday 9 am* ('Gone to the Big City' was abandoned as it might encourage thieves.)				The note was written on the blackboard and the children wrote it on paper. Two were chosen; one for the front door and one for the back door.
	All signed names or made marks.		3	3	
	Teacher moves the story forward with a physical activity. Horses, donkeys, etc. are mounted and all head for the big city. (See page 142 for Voice-over.)		2	3	The previous work was very concentrated and static; they need to move.
Teacher: Children: Child:	'What do you see over there?' Answers included: houses, smoke, tall buildings, a church. 'It's a long way away.'	16	2	3	
Teacher:	'Why are those soldiers standing over there?'	17	3	3	This question was not considered in terms of Personal Engagement. It was an irrelevant question whereby the teacher tapped into her knowledge of the book. Soldiers have connotations of danger from TV viewing.

Who asks	Description	Question number	Level of Personal Engagement	Category of Identification	Notes
	Children all crowded round the teacher who stated, in an attempt to rescue the lesson, 'I expect they are keeping the roads safe for travellers.'			1	
Child C:	The children accepted this, waved to the soldiers and rode happily into the town. 'Where can we leave our horses?'	18	3	3	Child indicates she is back in role as one on a journey.
Child C:	Answering own question, 'In that stable'. Teacher becomes the stable owner and takes the horses in demanding $2 from each child.				Young children readily accept teacher in, out and changing roles.
Teacher:	'How much do we have left?'	19	2		
	Children calculate that they now have $8 left.				
	On arriving at the city the children pointed out places recorded in their drawings. Some pointed to the actual drawing.		2	3	
	One child pointed to the market.		3	3	

Who asks	Description	Question number	Level of Personal Engagement	Category of Identification	Notes
Teacher:	'Shall we stay together or go in groups and come together later?' (Time on the clock in the classroom was noted.) The class decided to stay together.	20			This was dangerous as the teacher did want them to stay together.
Teacher:	Teacher changes role from one of the group to a specific role in the market. 'Apples are 5¢ each. Would you like one?'	21	2		Teacher picks up on child's contribution.
Teacher:	All buy one or some. 'Where have you come from?'	22		1/3	'Shopping' is a lovely game.
Teacher:	'Why are you visiting us today?'	23	3	3	Most children answered in context.
Child B:	Many different answers here, for example: 'We are tailors and we are here to buy cloth.'		3	4	
Teacher:	'I wonder which of you made my new coat?'	24			Teacher's question is used to reinforce in some and build in others a commitment to the drama.
Children:	'We all did.' (Actually it was 'I did' in chorus!)				
Teacher:	'All at the same time?' (This led to an argument; she monitored and intruded only in role.)	25	3	1	The teacher in role as 'the one who doesn't know' (see page 46).

Who asks	Description	Question number	Level of Personal Engagement	Category of Identification	Notes
Teacher: (to one child)	'Didn't I hear you say you made the collar?'	26	2/3		Restored order by focusing on one child.
	Eventually the children agreed on who had contributed what and the class decided it was time to eat.		3	3	
	A break for ten minutes. The children continued to play 'market' and decided to go to the 'restaurant'.		3	3	The teacher makes menus with prices during the break.
	The teacher, in role as restaurant owner, welcomed the children, seated them, offered the menu, took orders, served food.		2	1	Activity was used to develop social skills in restaurants.
Teacher:	'I hope you've enjoyed your meal. Here is your bill.' The teacher recognized that the children needed support and changed role. (With older children she would have remained as restaurant owner.)	27		4	Not a question but a statement to stimulate questions. This statement demands a high level of thinking.
Teacher:	'How much do we owe?' Child who can read figures reads them out.	28		3	This question allies her with the tailors' concern.

Who asks	Description	Question number	Level of Personal Engagement	Category of Identification	Notes
Teacher: Children:	'How much money have we spent?' So much on horses, apples, and individual items.	29	2	3	
Teacher:	'How much money do we have left?'	30	3		Had it been more, the drama would have changed.
	Group worked out what they had spent and subtracted it from what they had originally. It was less than the bill total.	31	3	2	
Child:	'What are we going to do?'		4		
	Children made suggestions. (a) Repair the restaurant owner's clothes (b) Make new tablecloths (c) Run away		3/4 4	3	
Child:	'They know where we live. We told them.'	32	4	3	Child deals with 'easy' solution! (c)
Teacher:	'What will we use to buy food if we aren't earning money making clothes?'		5	4	The question here had to be extended for some but most grasped the significance.
Child A:	'Some can stay here and some of us can go home.'	33	3	3	
Teacher:	'How will we choose who stays and who goes?'		4		Teacher pressing.
	Discussion led to suggestion to draw lots.		3	3	

Who asks	Description	Question number	Level of Personal Engagement	Category of Identification	Notes
Teacher:	'I have children so I must go home.'		3	3	Teacher keeps pressure on.
	Four children volunteered to work for the restaurant because they had no families. One of these had a dog and another child offered to feed it.				
Child D:	'They might put us in jail.'		4		
Child B:	'What will our families do?'	34	4	3	Child is aware of implications.
	Children discussed this and decided that all would go home but four would return the next day.				
Teacher:	'How will you tell the restaurant owner?'	35	3	3	
	When the decision was made to ask him to come and talk to them because they had something to tell him, the teacher again took on the role of the restaurant owner.				
	He listened to their confession and their solution in silence.				
Teacher:	'Will you give me all the money you have left?'	36	3	3	Teacher tried to press, but only child C was involved.
Child C:	'We will give you some of it.'		4	4	

Who asks	Description	Question number	Level of Personal Engagement	Category of Identification	Notes
	Restaurant owner accepted the offer and left. She returned as one of the group taking the role of The Absentee (see page 46).				
Child E:	'How will he know that we will come back?'	37	5		This is a high order of thinking for a five-year-old.
Child F:	'My Dad signs his name.' (No prompting by the teacher)		4	1	The child has found the symbolic meaning but is not conscious of the dramatic form.
	The teacher, with the help of the children, drew up an IOU. All the children signed or made appropriate marks. One child was chosen to give it to the restaurant owner.				
	Everyone left with some promising to return the next day.		3	3	
	The homeward journey was much slower.				
	At the suggestion of the teacher they sat at the side of the road while the horses drank from the river.			1 and 3	Both children and 'tailors' were tired!
Teacher:	'I wonder if we made the right decision?'	38	6		Rhetorical question encouraging reflection. The drama ended here.

Who asks	Description	Question number	Level of Personal Engagement	Category of Identification	Notes
	The next day, the teacher, at the request of the children, read the story.		6		Reflective debriefing.
Child: (unprompted)	'Our story was better.'	39	6		
Teacher:	'Do you all agree?'				
	Nodding of heads.				
Teacher:	'Why do you think that?'	40	6		

Skill-building exercises for teachers
1   Select a story and develop questions that might be asked using the sub-headings in the chapter.
2   Rephrase the following questions to avoid 'Yes', 'No' and one word answers.
    (a)   Shall I go and complain to the Mayor?
    (b)   Do you think the Pied Piper will take the children away?
    (c)   Does the Mayor have a special place to sit?
    (d)   Shall we place an advertisement for a rat-catcher?
3   Rephrase the question, 'What shall we do now?'
     (i) to suggest tension
    (ii) to slow action
    (iii) to clarify
    in the following situations:
    (a)   The group, as archaeologists, have just discovered a tomb.
    (b)   A farmer has just learned that he has to go to the hospital for surgery, and the family is gathered in the kitchen.
    (c)   The group is confronted by a purple bottle labelled 'Do Not Open'.
4   Find the unanswered question in a story, poem or script, for example, in *Rumplestiltskin*, 'Why did he want the baby?'
5   Choose a fairy tale, myth, legend or folk tale and decide at what point you could stop reading to the class and what questions you could ask to promote engagement.
6   As number 5, but use a TV series. (They are with us, we might as well use them!)
7   Practise answering questions with a question, without repeating your partner's question. (You'll need an ally here.)
    For example:
    A: 'Are we going together?'
    B: 'Do you want me to come with you?'
    A: 'Isn't it necessary for us both to go?'
    B: 'How much do we have to carry?'
    A: 'You don't expect me to help, surely?'
    B: 'Have you forgotten I have a bad back?'
    and so on.
    See how long you can continue this by opening up possibilities for each other.
8   Work in groups of three where A records, B is the teacher and C is the student. All decide on a task. C begins the task. It is B's job, by skilful questioning, to deepen C's under-

standing of the task. Upon completion, A leads the discussion and analysis, using her notes.

9   In groups of three where A is the teacher, B is the student and C is the recorder. It is A's job, by skilful questioning, to get B into dramatic activity. C records all the questions and answers for later review and discussion. The starting point could be:

A: 'What do you want to make a play about?'

10   There are 40 questions asked in *The Three Poor Tailors*. Analyze each one to see what kind of question it is. Discuss which questions are the most important.

11   Rephrase the following in role questions to discover the out of role instruction, for example:

In role: 'Trooper John, will you ride at the back of the wagon train to round up the stragglers?'

Out of role: 'John, if you can't behave, you'll have to sit over there.'

(a)   'Who will take on the responsibility for transcribing our deliberations?'

(b)   'Our needs are different. Could every family discuss their priorities?'

(c)   'Will those of you who have returned from the hunt tell us of the dangers you overcame?'

(d)   'What is your greatest concern at this time?'

(e)   'I thought we had agreed to obey the commandment, "Thou shalt not kill"?'

References

1   Taba, Hilda, *Teacher's Handbook for Elementary School Studies*, 1967
2   Bolton, Gavin, *Towards a Theory of Drama in Education*, p 41
3   O'Neill, Cecily and Lambert, Alan, *Drama Structures*, p 141, Hutchinson, London, 1982
4   Davies G., *Practical Primary Drama*, 1983
5   Wagner, B. J., *Dorothy Heathcote*, p 90
6   Evans, David R., Hearn, Margaret T., Uhlemann, Max, Ivey, Allan E., *Essential Interviewing*, pp 54, 55, 77–80, Brooks/Cole, Monterey, California, 1979
7   O'Neill, Cecily and Lambert, Alan, *Drama Structures*, p 141, Hutchinson, London, 1982
8   O'Neill, Cecily and Lambert, Alan, *Drama Structure*, p 141, Hutchinson, London 1982

9 Ferguson, Marilyn, *The Aquarian Conspiracy*, ch. 9, Houghton Mifflin Co., 1980
10 Ambrus, V. G., *The Three Poor Tailors*, Harcourt Brace Inc., New York, 1965

5

Strategies and techniques

There are certain strategies and techniques that a teacher can employ to engage the students at both the thought and feeling level. The greatest difficulty is deciding which is strategy and which technique.

After consulting education, business, the military, law and medicine, we realized that there was no clear agreement on a definition for 'strategy' and 'technique'. We define them as follows:

Strategy: The frame through which the students will be taken into the action and the means by which they will explore the dramatic focus.

Activity: The strategy in action, or what the students will do.

Technique: The devices the teacher uses to implement the strategy.

Although strategy, activity and technique are linked by this definition, the teacher must see them as separate elements in her planning. Strategy and technique are the means by which the activity is made significant for the students.

It is interesting to note that many of the devices used by drama teachers can operate as strategy, activity or technique. This is shown in the following example:

Interview as strategy

Strategy	Activity	Technique
Interview where the dramatic focus is making questions.	In groups of three, work out a series of questions for a talk show.	Instruction

[handwritten note in right margin: ✓ WRITE IN JOURNAL]

Interview as activity

| Role drama whose topic is finding Atlantis. | *Interviewing* in pairs: A is a suspicious local fisherman, B is a deep-sea diver. | Instruction |

Interview as technique

| Mantle of the Expert, as deep-sea archaeologists. | Examining artifacts from a sunken ship. | Teacher in fringe role, *interviews* the experts for a news programme. |

In the classifications which follow, it is very important to keep in mind the flexible nature of strategy, activity and technique. Our aim in the classifications was to clarify those teaching devices which we have observed in operation and which we have found to be integral to our teaching.

Strategies

In classifying frames for action we have identified them by orientation. The first group are those strategies which are generally associated with the development of expressive skills. The second are concerned with developing interpretive skills. Group three deals with those strategies peculiar to role playing and the last group describes those strategies where role, interpretation and expressive skills must be employed for effective exploration.

After each of the descriptions we have listed a few books and journals which we have found useful, interesting and thought-provoking. Although one or two of the books might appear to be theory rather than practice, all are full of classroom activities.

Expressive frame orientation

General function: to develop the expressive instrument (physical).

1 Games

The teacher should be aware that a game has more uses than simply as a warm-up activity. It can be used diagnostically to assess the social health of the class. It can be used to develop group skills. It can function as an analogy: *Musical Newspapers* is an analogy for overcrowded conditions, *The Hunter and the Hunted* is an analogy which crystallizes the feelings of a spy on the run. A game can demonstrate a concept in a docudrama or anthology, for example, 'Pat-a-Cake' in a docudrama about The Holocaust. What we should never forget is that games are another way of looking at the human condition. They display 'in a simple way the structure of real-life situations'.[1]

Recommended reading
1 Opie, Iona and Opie, Peter, *Childrens Games in Street and Playground*, Oxford University Press, London, 1969
2 Fluegelman, A., ed., *New Games*, Doubleday, New York, 1976
3 Fluegelman, A., ed., *More New Games*, Headlands Press, Inc., California, 1981
4 Orlick, Terry, *Cooperative Sports and Games Book*, Pantheon Books, New York, 1982

2 Movement exercises

Although movement exercises help to develop the expressive instrument, they can also be taken into the meaning frame. *Mirrors* done with mothers and daughters revealed the reluctance of the mothers to give up responsibility for leadership to their daughters. Veronica Sherbourne's exercise of opening a curled-up body became the starting point in a role drama about passive resistance.

Movement is as much about stillness and making form as it is about shifting in space and changing form.

Recommended reading
1 King, Nancy, *Giving Form to Feeling*, Drama Book Specialists, New York, 1976
2 Boorman, Joyce, *Dance and Language Experience with Children*, Longmans, Canada, 1973
3 Nicholls, Bronwen, *Move!*, Heinemann Educational Books, London, 1979

3   Depiction

(Also known as tableau, still photograph, statue(s), freeze frame)
The teacher uses this strategy to look at what the students are
thinking, so a depiction is 'concretized thought'.

Depiction can also be used diagnostically to discover what
the students understand by, for example, exploration. If their
pictures are about death, destruction and jolly times at sea, the
teacher knows that 'the play for the teacher' will include
boredom, discomfort and homesickness.

Depiction can be used to reveal the specific in the general,
so the specific can become the material for the next part of the
drama. For example, the general context is arrival in a new land.
The students define the specific by making a picture at the
moment of completing disembarkation, which is the cutting of
the last link with the old. If, in the depiction, they are looking
back to the ship, it will be a different role drama from one that
is built on looking forward to the new land.

Depiction is an excellent means of solving 'the disaster
problem'. Disasters are rightly seen by students as exciting drama
sources, but you cannot turn the classroom into an erupting
Mount St Helen's! However, you *can* make a picture of the
moment the volcano blows, and the feeling quality will be much
stronger in the depiction than if they tried to 'live through' the
experience (see Bolton, *Towards a Theory of Drama in Education*, p
44, Longman, 1979).

Depiction is also a way of showing change: 'How we were
and how we are now' (see Chapter 1, page 12).

Recommended reading
1   Barton *et al*, *Nobody in the Cast*, Academic Press, 1969, pp 44–
    47
2   Byron, Ken and Griffin, Dierdre, 'Still Image', *ABCDE Journal*,
    Vol. 5, No. 2, December 1983

4   Dance drama

This is not ballet or even modern dance! It is simply moving,
sometimes individually, but more usually as a small group or
with the whole class, interpreting a story or theme to a piece of
music. When students are older, dance drama can be used as a
means of finding concrete expression for abstract ideas, for
example, a dance drama prepared for a Remembrance Day
assembly.

Recommended reading
1 Boorman, Joyce, *Creative Dance in the first three grades*, Longman Canada, 1969
2 Boorman, Joyce, *Creative Dance in Grades 4 to 6*, Longman Canada, 1971
3 Leese, Sue, Palmer, Moira, *Dance in Schools*, Heinemann Educational Books, 1980
4 Lynch, Fraser, *Dance Play, Creative Movement for very young children*, New American Library, New York, 1982

5 Mime

We are not referring to mime as the sophisticated, technically demanding art form, but as a means of developing in students the ability to 'sign' with confidence. For example, the head of an Ethiopian family does not have to have a real jug to dip it into the well.

The constraint that mime places on language permits a shy class to explore ideas which they can then talk about, and it forces a very verbal class into other ways of expressing thought and emotion.

According to Stewig, drama is spontaneous *oral* communication[2] but the power of gesture without words can stimulate language – another paradox!

Recommended reading
1 Hamblin, Kay, *Mime, A playbook of Silent Fantasy*, Doubleday, New York, 1978
2 Stolzenberg, Mark, *Exploring Mime*, Sterling Publishing Co. Inc., New York, 1983
3 Avital, Samuel, *Mime Work Book*, Lotus Light Publications, Wisconsin, 1982

6 Sound (non-verbal)

> drama is language . . . language in its very broadest sense . . . as a non-verbal/verbal code for encapsulating and sharing experience.[3]

Non-verbal sound work is more than just creating noise. Playing with sound is tremendous fun, and more than this, it is a way of 'looking' at the world through your ears. Whether it is finding how many sounds you can make with your body, or creating an instrument of your own design, or translating pictures of sounds into the sounds themselves, or making a 'soundscape' or a 'sound poem', or researching the Doppler effect, or creating the Taj Mahal in stereophonic sound, the student is developing his sensitivity to sound, his appreciation of the significance of silence, his awareness of sound as a theatrical element and, above all, he is honing his listening skills.

Recommended reading
1   Schafer, R. Murray, *When Words Sing*, Berandol Music, Toronto, 1967
2   Schafer, R. Murray, *Ear Cleaning*, Berandol Music, Toronto, 1967

7   Sound (verbal)
We do not use sound exercises specifically to develop the vocal instrument. A lot of the voice work which appears in curriculum resource guides can be harmful unless taught by a qualified voice specialist. Training the voice, like training to be an expert in mime, needs consistent daily application over a number of years.

> The training of the voice is the most difficult and time-consuming of all theatre disciplines. Voice formation should continue for the entire four years of the training, since, without such an extended training, it is, in most cases, quite impossible to achieve any real control. It should be stressed that the actor's vocal faculties must be continuously exercised . . . .[4]

However, drama is about communicating, so appropriate language, clarity of speech and expression, and an ability to match words to intention are important. Lots of experience of speaking as others through role is the sort of training we recommend.

If you have something important to say, you will make sure it is heard. It is the teacher's responsibility to see that drama provides students with situations and roles of significance where what is happening is so important that the participants are impelled to speak.

Recommended reading
1   Berry, Cicely, *Your Voice and How to Use it Successfully*, Harrap and Co., London, 1975
2   Crampton, Esme, *Good Words Well Spoken*, Norman Press, Toronto, 1980

Meaning frame orientation

General function: the development of language to express thought and emotion.

1 Discussion

The key to lively discussion, whether in or out of role, is the teacher's ability to pose the right question which initiates the discussion (see Chapter 3). If the teacher uses discussion in role, she must be aware of maintaining the dramatic interest in a basically inactive activity.

The teacher can use discussion to sort out ideas, plan ahead, evaluate, or reflect. Discussions are free-flowing interactions in which everyone should have an opportunity to contribute.

The meeting

A meeting offers more control than a general discussion, because it always has a particular focus. A meeting is called to solve a problem, make a decision, or present information which will then be discussed.

For example, the class are sitting in a circle. The teacher asks them to imagine that they are in a meeting place in a small town in the Mid-West. Perhaps it is the schoolroom or a church hall. She explains that she will be taking part in the next activity. She introduces herself as a representative of the government. She has come to tell them about the opportunities which await them if they are prepared to make the long journey to Oregon. The government will give them free farming land and the country is extremely fertile. They will be much more prosperous if they decide to move.[5]

A meeting is more formal than a discussion and often requires a change of space or furniture arrangement.

An element of tension is added if the meeting is held in secret.

The confrontation

In any meeting conflicting opinions can cause a confrontation but it will not be a real confrontation unless the participants have strong feelings and informed opinions. The teacher must ensure that each side has had time to develop a strong commitment to the situation as well as plenty of facts to support their arguments. Heathcote says she never allows a group to split until each side has had a chance to experience what it is like on the other side.

Recommended reading
1   O'Neill, Cecily and Lambert, Alan, *Drama Structures*, Hutchinson, London, 1982, has many examples of discussion and meetings, as does *Dorothy Heathcote: Drama as a Learning Medium*,
2   Johnson, D. W. and Johnson, F. P., *Joining Together: Group Theory and Group Skills*, Prentice Hall, Inc., New Jersey, 1975, has some excellent exercises to help students develop their discussion skills.

2   Interview

This strategy promotes question-making on the part of the participants, rather than solely on the part of the teacher. The teacher should remember that the preparation of questions is an important preliminary activity which can be done in or out of role, collectively on the board, in pairs, or individually. For examples of different kinds of interview and the roles appropriate for interviewing see Chapter 3, pages 107 and 108.

Recommended reading
O'Neill, Cecily and Lambert, Alan, *Drama Structures*, 'Young Offenders', pp 173–179, Hutchinson, London, 1982

3   Story

The act of making a story is usually private when it is being written. However, a story which is written down can become a source for reading aloud by the story-maker or another. Story work requires at least two participants, the reader/teller and the listener.

Story-telling
The responsibility for sustaining the narrative and giving it shape, whether it is from the student's own experiences or from experiences that have happened to others, rests with the story-teller. Story-telling is not just giving factual information (a report) but should also involve elaboration so that it captures and sustains the interest of the listener. These same criteria of logic and interest apply when the student has to tell a story that is based on a source which he has read. For example, tell the story of Hansel and Gretel as if you were the witch.

Reading a story aloud

The most important aspect of this strategy is that it introduces the student to the constraints of working with other people's ideas and words rather than his own. Teachers should be aware of the need to provide students with sources rich in language-modelling opportunities. Reading stories to others is a preliminary step to working with scripts. However, the narration in a story supports and elaborates the dialogue, whereas in a script the dialogue stands alone and it is the student's responsibility to provide the elaboration for himself.

Recommended reading

1   Morgan, John and Rinvolucri, Mario, *Once Upon a Time: Using Stories in the Languages Classroom*, 1983
2   Chilver, Peter and Gould, Gerard, *Learning and Language in the Classroom: Discursive Talking and Writing Across the Curriculum*, Pergamon Press, Oxford, 1982
3   Barton, Robert, *Tell Me Another*, Pembroke, Markham, 1986

4   Monologue

Monologue is another form of story-telling. James Moffett defines it as one person sustaining both sides of the conversation. Unlike soliloquy, a monologue is always addressed to someone, who may react but not interrupt. This strategy, with its strong theatrical demands, is a great challenge to the student. He must be able to remember lines and be prepared to be the focus of attention. The pressure can be reduced and the interest level maintained for the rest of the class if they have been put into an appropriate listening role. For example, T. S. Eliot's *Journey of the Magi* could be delivered as if the speaker were a servant of one of the Kings and the listeners were in role as his grand-children.

> 'A cold coming we had of it,
> Just the worst time of the year
> For a journey, and such a long journey:
> The ways deep and the weather sharp,
> The very dead of winter . . .'

Or the opening paragraph of Daphne DuMaurier's novel *Rebecca* need not be delivered by the second Mrs DeWinter but could be read as an excerpt from a patient's diary as part of an address given by a Freudian psychoanalyst at a conference.

'I dreamt I went to Manderley again. It seemed to me I
stood by the iron gate leading to the drive, and for a
while I could not enter for the way was barred to
me . . .'[6]

The teacher should monitor the selections to ensure that the
material has potential. The act of justifying his choice gives the
student opportunities to deepen the meaning for himself. His
challenge is to discover his role as speaker and to define for his
peers their roles as listeners. There will often be an improvised
opening to enable the speaker to slide into the monologue. For
example:

'So! You want to hear the story of the journey I took so
many years ago again? Well, 'a cold coming we had of
it . . .'

Then everyone can slide into dramatic playing through interaction at the end of the monologue.

Recommended reading
1   Moffett, James, *A Student-Centered Language Arts Curriculum,
    K-13*, Ch. 22, Houghton Mifflin Co., Boston, 1968
2   Any collection of first person transcriptions such as *10 Lost
    Years* or *Six War Years*. There is a good selection in *Words on
    Work*, Nemiroff *et al*, Globe/Modern Curriculum Press,
    Toronto, 1981

5   Script
This strategy is used to give students an opportunity to explore
scripts without the pressure of having to present a finished
product. When working in this way, the students must find the
meaning and then find ways to manifest that meaning through
the bare bones of the dialogue. Therefore the teacher must see
that the students operate not only as performers but also as
playwrights, directors and audience.
    This exploration includes:

(a) *examining*: for example, the students examine minimum
     scripts of short unassigned lines of dialogue and must
     improvise around these to find the many situations and
     roles inherent in the scripts.
        Hello.

Hello.
What are you doing?
Can't you tell?
Oh.

(b) *analyzing*: students are given a page of dialogue where the character allocations have been removed. Their task is to discover how many people are in the scene, what the scene is about and then who is saying the lines.

(c) *interpreting*: examining and analyzing scripts can lead to selecting one exploration and developing it into a scene (playwright), rehearsing it (director and performer) and sharing it with others (performer and audience).

The teacher can take an appropriate scene and ask students to interpret it as a dance drama, develop an unwritten scene, create a character collage, design the set, select one essential prop for each character. These activities build meaning and provide a repertoire of rehearsal techniques in preparation for later work in docudrama and anthology.

Recommended reading
1 Lundy, Charles, Booth, David, *Interpretation: Working with Scripts*, Academic Press, Canada, 1983
2 Barton, Robert, *et al*, *Nobody in the Cast*, Academic Press, Canada, 1969

Role playing

General function: the interaction of the expressive and meaning frames at the explorative level.

1 Simulation
This is a strategy used for training in life skills. It is a carefully planned series of exercises. The skills that are acquired will be employed in real life situations. For example, young children in a simulated visit to the ice cream shop, learn how to behave on a bus, how to ask for an ice cream, how to pay for it and how to operate as a well-mannered group; Crisis Line trainees are put into simulations to employ information and skills they are developing for handling phone calls.

Simulation is non-threatening because it is done in a safe situation like all role playing, and it helps students to go through the real situation with confidence. Teachers must be aware that although it does put students into role, or into an imagined situation, it is more akin to re-enacting a story than creating a role drama.

Recommended reading
1   Taylor, John L., Walford, Rex, *Simulation in the Classroom*, Penguin Papers in Education, Middlesex, 1972
2   Johnson, D. W., Johnson, F. P., *Joining Together: Group Theory and Group Skills*, Prentice Hall Inc., New Jersey, 1975

2   Dramatic playing

In dramatic playing the student is involved in activities which do not necessarily require him to be anyone other than himself. These activities are designed to place the student in a make-believe situation in which he can explore his reactions and actions in a spontaneous way. This strategy is non-threatening to both teacher and students because it is so open. The student can react using his own experience and is free from the constraint of worrying about how to put someone else's words in his own mouth.

Story is often used to initiate dramatic playing. David Booth used the device of putting the student in the story by reading *Sunflight* (the story of Daedalus and Icarus by McDermott), closing the book and asking, 'Did anyone see him fall?'

Another safe dramatic playing activity is sitting-down drama (see Chapter 2, page 26).

In either of the above examples the students are not required to get out of their seats until, and unless, they themselves suggest it.

Other sources besides stories which initiate dramatic playing are pictures, objects and improvisation exercises.

Recommended reading
1   Way, Brian, *Development through Drama*, Longmans, London, 1967
2   Davies, Geoff, *Practical Primary Drama*, Heinemann Educational Books, London, 1983
3   Bolton, Gavin, 'The activity of dramatic playing', *Issues in Educational Drama*, pp 49–63 (Day, C. and Norman, John, eds), The Falmer Press, New York, 1983

3   Mantle of the Expert

The students, though still themselves, are required to look at the situation through special eyes (see Chapter 2, page 31 and

Chapter 6, pages 174 to 175). The work here is about a task-oriented situation, where the job in hand must be done first. So doing the job is the vehicle that starts the creative ideas flowing.

Students in Mantle of the Expert do not have to have 'expertise'. Six-year-olds can be archaeologists. All that is required is that the task be done seriously and responsibly as any professional would do it. It is this attention to the task which protects the students from worrying about what they sound or look like.

Mantle of the Expert is a wonderful strategy for a group of mixed ages, provided the expertise is unknown (particularly to the older participants). It makes a successful Parent Evening activity because in it the students, having had experience in this strategy, will be able to 'teach' their parents. For example, older students had been working in a role drama about an alien civilization. Their parents became the first settlers from Earth. The in-role discussion which developed, about maintaining a clean environment on the planet, certainly demonstrated to the parents the quality of work and skills demanded by their children's drama programme.

Recommended reading
1   Although to date there is no book specifically about Mantle of the Expert, it is Dorothy Heathcote's strategy, and is demonstrated all through *Dorothy Heathcote: Drama as a Learning Medium*. O'Neill and Lambert use it extensively in *Drama Structures* and Tarlington and Verriour define it neatly in *Offstage*.
2   Heathcote, D., Herbert, P., 'A Drama of Learning: Mantle of the Expert', *Theory into Practice*, vol. 24, no. 3, Summer 1985

4   Role drama
A role drama is also known as a contextual drama, a role play or a drama structure. Role drama is the unfolding of a series of events which make up a story, although the story cannot be 'written' until the exploration is completed.

> 'It is the strategy which is most likely to achieve the kind
> of change in understanding which is at the heart of
> educational drama.'[7]

Role drama is an umbrella strategy which makes use of a wide variety of other strategies, together with the appropriate teaching techniques. This allows the teacher and students to work over an extended period of time. This also enables them to explore the ideas and themes from many perspectives, thereby building volume.

In role drama, the teacher is inside the work much of the time, working in role.

Recommended reading
1 O'Neill, Cecily and Lambert, Alan, *Drama Structures*, Hutchinson, London, 1982
2 O'Neill, C. *et al*, *Drama Guidelines*, Heinemann, London, 1976
3 Wagner, Betty Jane, *Dorothy Heathcote: Drama as a Learning Medium*, National Education Association, Washington, 1976
4 Linnell, Rosemary, *Approaching Classroom Drama*, Edward Arnold, London, 1982

5 Improvisation
Improvisation should not be confused with 'improvs' and 'skits' which suggest activities that take place without the teacher and which are generally of a superficial nature, drawing upon the stereotype.

Improvisation should be seen as a strategy which develops spontaneity. 'It is here that (the student) will find the relationship between the reality of his own inner life, both intellectual and emotional, and its physical expression, the means through which he can convey this reality to others.'[8]

Improvisation consists of activities of an exercise nature, based upon source, in which the teacher does not participate in role, but stays outside the action, facilitating the work through side-coaching. Sometimes she can build volume by taking on a fringe role. The challenge for the students is to use the information given on who, what, when, where, and how, to discover, through improvising, the why? For example:

> 'I divided them into family groups, so that they were working separately from each other, each family having its own son, as it were, who was in this condition. The moment of interaction had to be carefully selected and what I did was to choose a moment when they visited him in hospital, when he had recovered from the operation but was, in fact, physically quite helpless and mentally very unstable and defective. Now, I didn't know how they would cope with direct eyeball-to-

eyeball interaction, so I simply set it up in context, but as a kind of exercise, whereby we assumed that, when they came across their son in the hospital, he was attempting to tie his shoelace and failing – so that the whole focus of concentration of that family was on helping him to tie that shoelace. We held some discussions before we did the exercise on the extent to which one should help in those kind of circumstances where the helping really is encouraging him to tie the shoelace, or in fact, doing it for him.'[9]

There is often an out of role discussion to preplan the scene, as illustrated above. The teacher must be careful that the students do not talk the whole thing through so that spontaneity is lost and they are merely trying to remember what it was they planned to do.

Recommended reading
1   Lundy, Charles and Booth, David W., *Improvisation*, Academic Press, Canada, 1985
2   Johnstone, Keith, *Impro*, Methuen, London, 1981
3   Saint-Denis, Michel, Chapter 6 in *Training for the Theatre*, Suria Saint-Denis ed., Theatre Arts Books, New York, 1982. Although the chapter is entitled 'Silent Acting – Improvisation', what the author has to say about the act of improvising with or without words is worth reading.

Theatre genres

General function: the interaction of the expressive and the meaning frames, using the communication of others to develop interpretative skills.

The teacher will recognize the time when her students need the challenge of bringing to life other people's words, as well as their own, by applying the skills they have developed. The main skill being the ability to read! (Paradoxically, the poor reader can, with careful guidance on the part of the teacher, develop his reading skills through his work with sources in drama.) Although the teacher often feels that she is not needed because she is outside the work, this is not the time for her to leave the students to 'go it alone'. The teacher's job is to introduce them to the source and to the particular conventions of the genre and then to guide them through their explorations, reminding them that the other strategies are the means by which they can discover the meaning inherent in the text. For example, non-verbal sound can support Choral Speaking by evoking memory; a series of dissolving depictions become the lens through which we find the themes in Reader's Theatre; story-telling is the foundation of Story Theatre; improvisation is a way to explore Chamber Theatre; Dance Drama is often the key to successful Choral Dramatization and every strategy can be a part of Ensemble Theatre.

1   Choral Speaking

Using a source which is rich in language, ideas and themes, the teacher works as conductor, soliciting from the class their ideas and suggestions for interpretation. Everyone does not have to speak at once. Pairs, small groups and individual voices may be used and they may speak, sing, whisper either responsively, antiphonally, repetitively or accompanying themselves with non-verbal sounds. The class may be divided into groups physically and some movement of a simple nature may be introduced. Choral Speaking can be an excellent way to join two classes together for a special occasion. For example, two classes of senior students worked separately on different parts of *A Child's Christmas in Wales* by Dylan Thomas. When they met they were surprised and delighted to discover that there were parts in which they all spoke together and the class responsible for the last few lines were accompanied by the other class softly humming Silent Night.

Recommended reading
Barton *et al*, *Nobody in the Cast*, pp 121–145.

2   Choral Dramatization

In this strategy, the class can be divided into groups of five or six, each group working on a different source. The devices of Choral Speaking are combined with movement to dramatize the source. Choral Dramatization is both aural and visual. The whole group can do both the speech and the movement, or various small groups can alternate movement and speech. It is important 'that the flow of the language, the rhythm, and the cadence of the speech is enhanced by movements which 'deepen the meaning of the writing.'[10]

An example of a source for Choral Dramatization is:

Death Rites II
The animal runs, it passes, it dies. And it is the great cold.
It is the great cold of the night, it is the dark.
The bird flies, it passes, it dies. And it is the great cold.
It is the great cold of the night, it is the dark.
The fish flees, it passes, it dies. And it is the great cold.
It is the great cold of the night, it is the dark.
Man eats and sleeps. He dies. And it is the great cold.
It is the great cold of the night, it is the dark.
There is light in the sky, the eyes are extinguished, the star
shines.
The cold is below, the light is on high.
The man has passed, the shade has vanished, the prisoner is
free!
Khvum, Khvum, come in answer to our call!

Gabon Pygmy, Africa[11]

Recommended reading
Lundy and Booth, *Interpretation*, pp 73–79.

3   Story Theatre
Invented by Paul Sills, this strategy involves the class or smaller
groups presenting a story in which both narrative and dialogue
are used, while at the same time the appropriate action is demonstrated. What is challenging here is to discover which character
says which parts of the narrative, the choice being made on the
basis of what most effectively conveys the meaning. For example:

> One day as Frog was walking along the path, he met
> Snake who asked him where he was going. Frog said,
> 'I am going to find some treasure'.
> 'Then I shall come too' said Snake, as she slithered from
> the rock immediately followed by her two children.
> They walked briskly in single file until they came to a
> gate . . .

There are several ways to script this as Story Theatre:

Frog:	One day as Frog was walking along the path . . .
Snake:	He met Snake. 'Where are you going?' asked Snake.
Frog:	'I am going to find some treasure', Frog said.
Snake:	'Then I shall come, too', said Snake as she slithered from the rock.
Snake's children:	'Us, too', said Snake's children, following close behind.

All:	They walked briskly along the path in single file until they came to a gate . . .

or

Frog:	They walked . . .
Snake:	Briskly along the path . . .
Snake's Child 1:	One after . . .
Snake's Child 2:	The other . . .
All:	Until they came to a gate . . .

Recommended reading
Lundy and Booth, *Interpretation*, pp 87–90.

4   Reader's Theatre

Like Story Theatre, both dialogue and narration are used, but Reader's Theatre is a 'theatre of the mind'. The movie should run in the audience's head and therefore movement is restrained and generally abstract in nature. Reader's Theatre is an excellent strategy for a class that is called upon to present to an audience before their acting skills have matured because the convention places more emphasis on meaning than on action.

In the following example, the students have to decide who it is that is afraid before they can decide how it should be said.

> The trainer fired his gun. He fired again, but Goliath was not frightened. He kept roaring and leaping right up against the cage, first in one place, then in another. Then in one great leap he hit the wire door. It swung back, and Goliath was out of the cage!
>
> The people in the stands screamed and tried to get out as fast as they could. The trainer inside the cage was busy keeping the other four lions under control. Nobody knew what to do about Goliath.
>
> The great animal stood there looking bewildered. He roared a great loud roar just to prove to himself he was not afraid.
>
> Then he began to creep slowly toward the aisle where the children were sitting.[12]

Recommended reading
1   Lundy and Booth, *Interpretation*, pp 80–86
2   Coger, Leslie and White, Melvin, *Reader's Theatre Handbook*, Scott Foresman and Co., Illinois, USA, 1973
3   For short excerpts suitable for Reader's Theatre: any of the three source books from *Colours, a language arts program*, Longmans Canada Ltd, 1974

5   Chamber Theatre

Chamber Theatre is a combination of Reader's Theatre and Story Theatre, in which each group is responsible for preparing a particular part of the story. The groups are set up in a circle so that they can all see each other. The first group begins. When they are finished the second takes over, like the pages turning in a book. Each group knows only a part of the story, so it is challenging and exciting to see the story unfolding and to make the adjustments needed as the group discovers more about their part in the story. Chamber Theatre can be a good way of preparing students for a public performance as it takes place, like chamber music, not for an audience, but for the pleasure of the participants. An example is 'The Last Night of the World' by Ray Bradbury, from Lundy and Booth's *Interpretation*.

6   Ensemble Drama

This strategy is Chamber Theatre 'writ large'! Groups of between ten and twenty people choose to work with a group leader on a particular task with a myth or folk tale as source. The tasks might be improvising, Story Theatre, Choral Speaking, Dance Drama, Reader's Theatre, singing chorus, orchestra, sound effects or visual effects. The group then goes off to prepare the excerpt from the story or, in the case of the orchestra, visual effects, or sound effects, to carry out the instructions given. They reassemble and, under the direction of the 'conductor', participate in the unfolding of the events in the story. This strategy is another good way of bringing a number of classes together for a special event, and has been used very successfully by its inventors, David Booth and Robert Barton at the Council of Drama in Education conferences in Ontario.

Although the organizing teacher or teachers do not participate other than by coaching from the sidelines and 'conducting', they must be prepared to spend time in structuring the material beforehand.

7 The Play

A play is a source for classroom drama and its potential is often overlooked by teachers because they see it as a product rather than a structure for student exploration. We are not talking about the play as a piece of literature, but as a source that has to be lifted off the page into dramatic action.

For example, a class of senior students spent a term exploring the *Antigones* of Sophocles and Jean Anouilh using many strategies:

- Interview: the two Creons were interviewed on a TV talk show.
- Dance Drama, Choral Dramatization and Choral Speaking were applied to the chorus of the Greek play and tried out with the speeches of The Chorus in the modern version.
- Script: the students re-scripted the poetic translation into contemporary speech and some attempted to put the contemporary into verse.
- Role drama: the students explored what would have happened if Antigone had obeyed Creon, and the teacher was asked to take on the role of Polynices back from the shades.
- Improvisation: a scene between Antigone and her father, Oedipus. In order to make this scene work, they had to research Greek tragedy and from that they began to understand more clearly how Anouilh was using Antigone as a metaphor for France under the German occupation in the Second World War.

In a production, most of these students would have been in the chorus, if anywhere, but as the play was used as a class project, all had an equal opportunity to explore this sophisticated material. They had been prepared for the material through previous drama work.

The teacher stood by (she had almost taught herself out of a job) but she was fully involved, not as a fountain but as a well into which the students could dip when they needed.

Recommended reading
1 Lundy and Booth, *Interpretation*, sections 8, 10 and 13: excellent sources for suggestions and materials for work in the above strategies (numbers 5, 6 and 7).

'Certainly we must make opportunity for the product to be concluded, probably with an audience, however small, but we must not overlook the fact that it is the making of the drama which is going to contribute most to the growth of the child.'

Dorothy Heathcote[13]

8   Anthology and Docudrama

In both these strategies although the intention is presentation, they are appropriate for classroom work because of their flexible and episodic nature. As in The Play (see page 126), the students explore themes and events using many methods. Furthermore, in both Anthology and Docudrama, the students are required to find an overall dramatic structure to contain their concepts, both for their own satisfaction and for the satisfaction of their audience.

Anthology
A series of short scenes, based on sources and developed around a theme, for example:
• It's OK to be different
• Everyone is a hero to someone
• Orphans

Docudrama
A series of short scenes based on an historical event or events and using as much primary source as is available: Jackdaws, journals, diaries, first-person interviews, photographs, newspapers, documents, lists and inventories are some of the sources to be researched. Possible titles are:
• Botany Bay
• Klondike Gold
• The Slave Trade
A docudrama can be made out of material much closer to home. 'Attic' docudramas can be developed from students' research into their own families and the town in which they live.

At the senior level, both strategies provide opportunities for all students to synthesize their learning and to test it out in a public forum. The teacher's function is that of 'inside critic' which combines the roles of Artistic Director (to monitor the aesthetic content) and Producer (to ensure a smooth operation). However, above all, she is *the teacher*, whose primary function is to promote learning for all her students.

Recommended reading
Lundy and Booth, *Interpretation*, sections 11 and 12.

9   Puppets, masks and craftwork

Puppets, masks and craftwork are often used by the teacher to demonstrate to parents and administrators that drama is being done. A puppet in the desk, a mask on the wall or a piece of craftwork in Father's office is no guarantee that any drama has taken place and, in our experience, it generally has not! However, they do have a place as interpretive devices through which the student can extend his understanding.

For example, puppets can encourage the development of language in a reluctant speaker. A mask can transform a thirteen-year-old into an all-powerful king. The drawing of a coat of arms can transport a student into the life of the court. The making of a totem pole can provide a history for the tribe.

It is not skilled manipulation that is important, it is the projection of the self into the object which justifies the use of these devices as strategies in a drama classroom.

We think the above strategies are particularly suitable in the post-Christmas period. As in the Mantle of the Expert, a good deal of learning can be achieved through attention to task. Students who have been working hard physically and mentally will appreciate the change to manual work, which requires the same attention of mind and body but in a different way.

Recommended reading
1   Currell, David, *Learning with Puppets*, Ward Lock Educational, London, 1980
2   Appel, Libby, *Mask Characterization: An Acting Process*, Southern Illinois University Press, 1982
3   Rolfe, Bari, *Behind the Mask*, Personabooks, California, 1977

Sharing, Showing and Demonstration

Sharing

There is always an element of 'showing' in the drama class because everyone is working in the presence of his peers and the teacher. At the exploration stage it is the teacher's responsibility to reduce the pressure of this awareness of being watched.

The best way to do this is to make sure that the task is clear and challenging, the material interesting, and the strategy and techniques appropriate, giving opportunities for engagement and commitment. Students are often required to 'show' their work before they are skilled enough to do it competently and to 'share' their work before they are confident enough to learn from the experience.

When the students are aware that their work is labelled 'drama' or 'theatre arts' their expectation will be to show it. They know that an actor 'shows' to an audience: 'Are we just going to *do* today or are we going to *show*?' This is beginning from where they are and it is unwise to ignore their needs. They see showing as a major part of drama. Of course, some just want to show off, but others have a genuine need to test out the validity of their work. After all, in most other subjects they have evidence of where they stand through marks received for essays and tests. We know that showing before they are ready is unproductive (not to mention embarrassing and boring) but it can be a happy experience for all if the teacher handles it properly. How? By making the showing part of the learning experience, so that it is seen as an element of the process, not the result.

For example, 'Let's look at this group's depiction of the slaying of the Gorgon to see how they solved the problem of where and how Perseus is standing.' The teacher is telling the audience what to look for and diffusing the evaluation element. The audience have been through the same process, so looking at other people's work will enable them to compare, pick up an idea or two and perhaps discover a new perspective which will deepen the meaning for them. The 'showers' are having the experience of presenting themselves and their ideas to others. For example 'Don't begin until both you and the audience are ready and make sure that you finish and don't just stop. You'll know what I mean.'

We define this kind of showing as *Sharing*.

Showing

Teachers can move their students into another kind of 'showing' when the skills, experience and confidence of the students are such that they are strong enough to withstand the critical feedback which will arise. The audience, too, will now be experienced in responding and it is the teacher's job to help them to give positive critical feedback.

The general criteria behind Showing are: respect for the material, appropriate use of the conventions, and clarity of

meaning. The general guidelines for feedback are: What worked
for you? and What things are you confused about?

The players are learning whether they have made explicit to
others what was obvious to them, thus evaluating themselves
and discovering that the audience response can be a part of their
work. This is the first step towards 6.3 of the Taxonomy (see
page 27).

Demonstration

The teacher who uses role drama as a means of illuminating
subjects in the curriculum (Drama as Method) or as a drama
strategy, may find her students are not expecting to show.
However, at appropriate times she may need to have them do
so in order to provide:

(a)   material for reflection
      'Would it be a good idea to look at this family a year from
      now to see how this incident has changed their lives?'

(b)   material for information
      'The teacher, working from a document about 19th
      century street children, asks the class to work in groups
      of five or six. The task is to prepare and show a short
      scene which will tell the rest of the class something about
      the way they have been living. Some of these scenes show
      the children living by their wits, while others show the
      poverty and violence of the homes some of them once
      knew. The teacher's comments afterwards encourage the
      class to consider the children's relationship with each
      other, their attitudes to authority, and the ways in which
      they cope with the hardships of their lives.'[14]

(c)   material for selection
      'In groups pupils devise a number of scenes showing an
      incident in which one of the hostel rules is broken . . .
      The pupils select one of the incidents shown for further
      inquiry.'[15]

(d)   a means of re-introducing material after a break
      In a role drama on immigration, the period ended when the
      students were being interviewed by immigration officers. In
      the next class, the teacher began by asking them to demon-
      strate the scene in each home where they discussed the
      interview they had had.

(e) a means of unifying the whole group after small group work
In a role drama about a hospital, the students are working in
their respective departments. The teacher stops the dramatic
playing and all departments in turn are asked to demonstrate what they are doing to deal with the emergency. At
the end of the demonstration she comments: 'It is obvious
that, despite the pressure of the crisis, we all share the same
concerns for the health of our patients.' (from Heathcote)

(f) a means by which the students can find and frame the
significant moments of their work
'Show me what we have just done as a scene from a film.
What would you want the viewer to see?'

To clarify:
Sharing is the exchange of work in progress.
Showing is the exchange of work which is ready for critical
feedback.
Demonstration is the sharing of work within a role drama.

Sharing, Showing and Demonstration are devices to present
student work. We have indicated some ways in which the teacher
can put these devices at the service of learning.

Ritual, Reflection and Distancing

General function: We have isolated these strategies because they
are powerful devices for taking students into commitment and
internalization; those levels of engagement which have the most
potential for 'shifts in understanding'. (Bolton, 1979)

In drama, as in real life, Ritual and Reflection are ways of crystallizing meaning. Distancing is the strategy which allows the
students to find the meaning in situations which may be too
close, emotionally painful or embarrassing for them to deal with.

1 Ritual
Ritual, by its highly structured form and economical nature (all
extraneous detail is cut away, every word and gesture must
count) binds meaning together for the group.
To use Ritual as a strategy – the frame through which the
students are taken into the action – we suggest the following
categories and activities. These activities can be done with the

whole group in action, or all the students in the action but
working independently, or an individual in action with the group
participating as spectators.

Departures	*Arrivals*	*Celebrations*
leaving on a journey	returning from a journey	burning the mortgage
preparing for battle	arriving in a new land	marriage*
death*		an anniversary
packing a suitcase	birth*	a banquet
arming oneself	unpacking a suitcase	a toast
the send-off		acknowledging achievements
	passing through immigration	a religious festival
	marking territory	
	a receiving line	

Dedications/Affirmations	*Procedures*
swearing allegiance	an operation
hoisting a flag	meeting
placating the gods	trial
initiation*	reading a will
swearing an oath	transferring property
signing a contract	taking an inventory
joining a society	calling the roll

*Traditional rites of passage

Ritual, because of its formal nature, is unhurried. The techniques the teacher employs are chosen because they help to delay
the action so that the participants may realize the full significance
of their actions.

Some techniques (page 139 *et seq.*) that can be used are:

- voice-over
- narration
- silence
- symbolizing
- minimalizing
- contracting
- teacher in role

Unless she is working with inexperienced students, the
teacher should take a role where she does not need to be the
centre of the action, but rather participates in a consulting role.

(a) 'The one who knows' (Authority, middle status) holds the history of the ritual, putting herself at the service of the group and forcing the students to question and evaluate her contributions.
Some possible roles are:

- the oldest inhabitant (the rituals of the tribe)
- the grandmother (the rituals of the family)
- the Professor Emeritus (the rituals of the profession).

With very young children, she may need to demonstrate a more obviously authoritative role, for example, the retiring captain of the ship, the distributor of medals, the Queen's old nurse.

(b) 'The one who does not know' (the Helpless, the Absentee; low or middle status) has been away, or has newly joined, or comes to see how things are done. The students are put in the position of having to clarify, explain, defend and teach.
Some possible roles are:

- Canadian astronaut at NASA.
- Cartier greeted by the first people of the New World
- Old doctor returning to medical school to observe the latest techniques in surgery as demonstrated by doctors in training.

(c) 'The inspector' slows down the action. The teacher then has an opportunity to provide a sense of significance so that the students may develop a stronger belief in their roles. For example:

> 'Let each immigrant stand beside his luggage and be prepared to open it for the Customs Officer. You have, no doubt, studied the list of those goods which are not permitted entry into our country.'

The strategy of Ritual and its techniques is well demonstrated in *Drama Guidelines* (O'Neill, 1976), Lesson 1, 'Sir Dominic'. For example:

> 'The time has come to choose. I shall walk around the circle and where my finger stops there is Sir Dominic.' The teacher walks slowly around the circle twice. There is real and mounting tension and excitement. "This is Sir Dominic, the chief of all my knights. Take your place on the right hand of your king."

2   Reflection

Reflection as a strategy is the exception which proves the rule. It is the frame through which the students are taken out of the action of the plot and enter the action of the theme. The following categories and activities are suggested to give the students an opportunity to reflect.

Writing
in role:
logbook
diary
casebook
letters
insert for a time capsule
first person story
reports
filling-in forms
newspaper stories
treaties or formal statements

out of role:
scripting
story writing

Reading
in role:
accounts of others who have
    had the experience
primary source material of
    someone with a similar
    experience
own diaries as someone else or
    self in the future
formal factual report on an
    experience of significance to
    the reader

out of role:
research
novels
short stories
history

Listening to
in role:
roll call of those who have
    gone before
prayer to the gods
taped message
scene in which the problem of
    the listeners is discussed by
    others ('All prisoners will be
    silent while I question this
    woman.')

out of role:
our drama experience narrated
    by the teacher (Linnell,
    1982)
silence (listening to your own
    thoughts)

Speaking
in role:
thoughts
story telling
explaining to an interviewer
reading aloud your own
    writing as the one to whom
    the writing is addressed
describing what has happened
    to someone who was not
    there

out of role:
discussion

Depicting
in or out of role:
making a still picture or improvising a past moment of crisis or
    achievement
creating a scene analogous to the drama experience
drawing a mural for the Hall of Memory
making an insert for a time capsule
creating a self portrait
creating a visual of what is to come or who is to be met
constructing symbols (the throne, the shield, the crown)

    Reflection should not be employed only at the end of a
drama experience (nor only at the end of a lesson). Reflection
during the drama can give the student an opportunity to synthesize the experience 'so far', giving him time, because he is
held back from plot action, to sort out the relationship between
himself and himself in role, and an opportunity to evaluate his
commitment to the drama.
Some possible techniques are:

- speaking thoughts
- the tangible
- summing-up
- creating atmosphere

Heightened language
It is not appropriate to use heightened language for out of role
discussion as it tends to distance rather than personalize.
Timing
Choosing the moment for reflection depends upon the teacher
recognizing when both the collective and the individual have
something to reflect upon.
Placing
For private reflection, the students need space to work independently. For public reflection, the teacher must decide the most
effective arrangement for communication, for example, 'Stay
where you are', 'Go to a private space' or 'All gather round'. She
must also be aware of herself in relation to the group and if and
how she will move amongst them.
Questioning
Questions asked in reflection have to be carefully selected. 'What
happened?', 'Wasn't that fun?', 'How do you feel?' do not
contribute to the students' understanding of the experience.

There are many areas about which the teacher can ask reflective questions:

(a) the plot: 'This is what I saw. Is this what you wanted us to see?'
(b) the meaning: 'Do you think we were right to try and make the aliens like us?'
(c) the feeling: 'What would you tell your grandchildren about this experience?'
(d) universalizing: 'I wonder if the aliens feel like the first people did when they saw the explorers landing on their shores?'
(e) personalizing: 'Can you remember a time when your life depended upon someone you didn't trust?'

Teacher in role
Although the teacher can use reflective techniques in almost any role she chooses, specific roles can limit the teacher's ability to promote reflection. For example, a teacher in role as the Pharaoh *should* inhibit the honest reflection of her slaves!

3 Distancing

Distancing is a means of detouring feeling to arrive at feeling. It is the strategy which allows the students to find meaning in situations which, by their immediacy, might inhibit exploration. 'The teacher must know when a class or an individual is ready to leap into a high-threat situation and will allow attention to be focused on himself, and when that attention must be deflected . . . to diffuse self-consciousness.'[16] The following categories and examples are some of the ways in which the teacher can work through this strategy.

Analogy
Detouring can be through time, for example: the Grade 2 (7-year-olds) curriculum is 'Our Community'. The teacher must find the means to help the children see that 'community' is not just the post office, school, streets and grocer's but a system based on relationships and priorities. She takes them into a space drama where they create their own community. She could as easily take them back to building a community as 'pioneers'.

Detouring can be through story, for example: an old area of the city is being redeveloped as town houses which the present inhabitants cannot afford. The teacher chooses a story which parallels the students' concerns – Jezebel, Ahab and Elijah.[17]

Detouring can be through 'what the students know', for example: a teacher was asked to work with a group of 8–9 year old students on sexual abuse. There had been many reports of such abuse in the national and local press and parents were expressing concern. The teacher's task was to find a way to open up the topic for discussion. After reading and consulting with the school councillor, she decided that the two most important things to be explored by the students were (a) privacy and (b) how to say 'no' to authority. The teacher knew that each child had a private locker in the school and that all of them demonstrated a belief that a grown-up is always right. She distanced through a role drama about a ship's captain who was generally a fair man, but who had been opening the crew's lockers in their absence. The students, as sailors, had to find a way to approach him. Their conclusion was 'Even though he had the power over us, we knew he was wrong and that gave us the strength to say "no".' From this the teacher was able to relate her students' experience in the role drama to the more immediate learning.

Projection
Detouring can be through task, for example: a couple whose relationship is about to be dissolved, talk while watching television (see also Chapter 1, page 11, number 19).

Detouring can be through training, for example: in a role drama about euthanasia, the teacher divides the class into 'care teams'. Each team practises the procedures so that 'the matter may be concluded with a maximum of efficiency'. One team is selected to demonstrate (without a patient) the entire procedure, including the pulling of the plug. This demonstration gives the students an opportunity to be involved in the issue at the action level as 'doers' or 'watchers'.[18]

Detouring can be through object, for example: a class of slow learners, working on an improvisation between a circus ringmaster and a clown who has performed badly, move quickly into insults and pointless argument:

'You're stupid!'
'No, I'm not!'
'I'll feed you with my fist!'

When two glove puppets, appropriately costumed, were created, the students 'became' the characters:

'I was late because my wife was ill.'
'You can have another chance.'

The class watched each pair share their scene, commenting on
the work and the language used. The distancing produced a
maturity of expression which was not available to the students
before. (We are indebted to Betty Mundy of Princess Elizabeth
Elementary School, Welland, Ontario, for this illustration.)

Demonstration
This is a means which allows the students *to see* how it was rather
than *to be* how it was.

Detouring can be through depiction, for example: 'Will you
now set up a family photograph as it once was before the accident? . . . Rearrange the photograph to contain Jerry (the accident victim) as he now is.' (See Chapter 1, page 12, number 24.)

Detouring can be through a scene, for example: the students
are asked to demonstrate in groups of five, their most successful
robbery. Teacher in role and students in role then ask questions
of the demonstrating group. (See Chapter 1, page 13, number 2.)

Representation
This is a means of allowing students to express their concerns
in a situation of heightened intensity without the pressure of
performing the scene. For example: 'I set up a situation whereby
the parents of the boy were to be interviewed by the doctor, who
was going to explain to them that the boy only had a 50/50 chance
of living . . . I wanted to conduct it and not live through it, and
so I set it up in a very formal manner. I was in role as the doctor
. . . but when I ushered in the two parents, I ushered in nobody,
and sat nobody on the two empty chairs facing me, with a semicircle of students sitting round those two chairs . . . (they) were
invited by me beforehand to be the voices of the two parents
sitting on the chairs, and they could, as those two parents, ask
the kind of questions they thought those parents would ask.
Notice the tenses I'm using here. The kind of questions those
parents would ask, not "you are" the parents, "you are" in this
state of anxiety, "you are" experiencing this interaction with the
doctor.'[19]

In discussing the strategies of Reflection, Ritual and
Distancing, we have given examples which demonstrate the wide
variety of techniques which can be employed in the operation of
a single strategy. What follows is an analysis of some of the
techniques which are available to the teacher.

Techniques
Techniques (often referred to as 'devices') are what the teacher
uses to realize the full potential of the strategies and to create
significant experiences for her students.

We begin by looking at those things which the teacher does
herself to help create an environment in which both drama and
learning can take place. We then classify the techniques by their
functions, and finish by describing some techniques which we
have found to be successful.

Creating atmosphere
In Chapter 1 we said 'If drama is about meaning, it is the art
form of the theatre which encompasses and contains that
meaning.' We identified elements of the theatre which the
teacher can use as tools to enhance the working atmosphere:
Focus, Tension, Contrast and Symbolization. In addition she
should also consider the following:

Language
The language the teacher uses provides the students with a
model of how to speak and how to use grammatical construction.
This 'heightened' language need not be pseudo-Quaker: 'What
hast thou done, mine hearty? Keepst thou still thy watch?'.
However, it should be clear, concise and literate: 'Has the watch
seemed long?'

The law of effective communication is that 'less is more'.
The teacher, if she talks too much, creates an audience, not an
atmosphere and, just as a salesman can talk himself out of a sale,
so a teacher can talk the students right past the moment of action.

Intonation
By her voice, the teacher creates an atmosphere where work can
take place. In out of role instruction, side-coaching, etc., her
voice must be vital, clear, and with the signals established so
that she does not have to shout. In role, the teacher's intonation
must support the role and the meaning. If the students want a
King of whom they are afraid, she must decide whether to give
them the sure voice of authority or whether speaking in a gentle
voice would generate richer learning.

Timing
The teacher must be aware of the shape of the lesson in combination with her educational objectives. The students should

always have time for reflection, debriefing, discussion and planning.

Pacing
The teacher must be able to adjust the planned strategy, techniques and activities so that the students' energy is harnessed to the work. Flexibility and variety are the spice of life, they are also the agents which help to make satisfying drama.

Setting
A supportive atmosphere includes the setting. Untidy classrooms with a confusion of furniture generally result in untidy and confused work. The teacher must consider the arrangement of the space, the use of levels (risers, boxes, etc.), the positions of herself and the group, and the effective use of light and sound.

Sharing self
The students must be made aware from the beginning of the year of the standards that are important to the teacher, and she should know when it is appropriate to share her values with them.

When the teacher makes a mistake, she must allow the students to see that she is aware of it and is prepared to admit it. This is a way of showing the students that 'to err is human . . .' and it allows both teacher and students to get on with the good stuff and not hang about trying to fix the unfixable!

An atmosphere of mutual respect and vitality in a workmanlike and supportive environment is the first step towards a good company feeling in the theatre and it applies equally to the classroom.

Classification of techniques by function

1 Slowing down

This holds back the action.
This technique is used:

- to stop the students moving along the plot line and leaving the meaning behind.
- to give the students an opportunity to reflect on what has happened.
- to give the students an opportunity to look at implications.

2 Filling-in
Filling-in provides essential information (be careful not to provide more than is needed!)
This technique is used when:

- the role drama can't move forward without the information.
- the information will maintain the honesty of the drama. Without it the students are only 'knocking their ignorance around' and the drama could deteriorate.
- the students ask for the information.

3 Building volume
This fills in the meaning frame.
This technique is used:

- to prevent the students from seeing their work as a series of actions (this applies as much to a class in movement exercise as to a class working in role).
- to generate opportunities for the students to think more deeply about who they are and why they are there (implications).
- to give opportunities for seeing the situation from a number of perspectives.
- to give the students opportunities for internalizing.

Building volume is a technique which promotes and sustains the interaction of the expressive and the meaning frames. Heathcote (1976) referred to this technique as 'deepening the drama' and Bolton (1979) saw it as a means of eliciting 'Type D' drama.

4 Crystallizing
In this technique the significant is selected and framed so that it can be attended to.
The technique is used:

- when the students need a focus for their attention.
- to provide moments which will act as keys to remembering the whole.
- to comment through the Universal or the Paradox to promote reflection.

5 Unifying
This brings the parts together.
The technique is used:

- to show students with divergent views what they have in common.
- to give a sense of the collective when students have been working independently.
- to identify a common purpose.
- to find the common thread which links the action.

We have ordered the techniques which follow to some degree, but there is no attempt to classify them, as most can be applied in any of the general classifications above. For example: the voice-over may be used to slow down, fill in, build volume, crystallize or unify. When a teacher has a good repertoire of techniques, there should be no rules to inhibit the flexibility of their use.

Techniques where the teacher uses language for specific purposes

1 Voice-over
Voice-over is when the teacher instructs in the present tense and the students carry out the instructions while she is speaking. For example:

> 'Look at the wagon. How much will it hold? . . . Look at what you plan to take. . . . What are you prepared to do without? . . . What can you leave behind? . . . Begin now to collect your things and pack them carefully . . .'

The function of the voice-over is to control plot and situation, but teachers must be aware of the Pavlovian connotations and leave room for the students' imaginative contributions.

2 Narration
Narration is recounting the events in a story. It may be quite brief, or it may be extended, particularly if used to unify a role

drama.[20] The teacher highlights key moments of the drama so that the students go over the narrated experience in their imaginations.

Like Voice-over, Narration can control plot and situation, but it can do much more. The teacher can use Narration to create atmosphere, build volume, crystallize, move plot line, upgrade language, upgrade student status, compress time, infuse tension and provide material for reflection. Unlike Voice-over, Narration is spoken in the past tense:

> 'Each man took his rations and found a place by himself.
> As he ate his meagre meal, he thought of all he had
> gone through that day – the fording of the river, the loss
> of the supplies, . . .'

As with Voice-over, Narration is a technique which must not be over-used or be so long that it becomes the teacher's story and not the students'.

3 Summing-up

Summing-up is a form of Narration. It is not necessarily done at the *end* of the drama, but is a useful technique for giving structure and form to work which has been loose or disjointed.

> 'Now, let's see where we've got to. The fort is built, the
> supplies are stored and the search party has not yet
> returned . . .'

This example would also serve the teacher who sums up to begin the next class, or to start the work again after an interruption.

Summing-up is also, of course, a technique for concluding work in which the teacher can highlight the significant points and allow students to reflect upon them. The teacher can, for example, read selections from the students' written reflective work.

Summing-up must be logical, unbiased (it describes what *was*) and valid. This is not the place for the teacher to add anything extra to make it 'interesting', unless she is summing-up for the purpose of having her students correct her.

4 The Report

This is a concluding Summing-up in which the teacher writes or reads a factual report of the events that have occurred so that the students can compare it with their own role writing (letters, diaries, for example). The contrast will demonstrate that under any 'cool' writing lies a dilemma which affects people's lives.

For example, the teacher reads the factual account of a journey up the North Saskatchewan River in 1894, reported in a newspaper of the day, following number 16 (A Day's Journey) from 'The Way West' (O'Neill and Lambert, *Drama Structures*, page 49).

5   Universalizing

This is the technique of summing-up in the meaning frame by using what is happening in the drama 'as an occasion to remind the group that all through time people have found themselves in the position that the group are in themselves at that moment'. Teachers use this transfer 'to help (students) identify with a wider range of other human beings throughout time'.[21]

For example, in a role drama about space exploration: 'I wonder if Columbus had the same doubts as we have had?'. After a dance drama: 'In all my travels through Ontario, I have never found a community, however small, that doesn't have a dance hall. Now I know why.'

Techniques to draw language out of students

1   Tapping-in

The teacher 'freezes' the work and moves through the group, placing her hand on each student's shoulder or head and saying, 'Tell me what you are feeling in your heart.' (see Chapter 1, page 12, number 23) or 'What are your concerns?' The placing of the hand, the length of contact and the amount of pressure is a matter of the teacher's sensitivity. Sometimes it is helpful if she does not withdraw her hand until the speaker has finished.

2   Voice collage

The students are in a relaxed groups, the teacher gives the instruction: 'Feel the moment when it is right for you to speak. Some may want to speak several times. You will know when it is right for you.' This calls upon the teacher's skill in waiting and knowing when to bring the activity to a close. The group may speak as individuals in role, or as the thoughts of one individual.

For example, the students speak the thoughts of a mother as she watches her daughter win a gold medal at the Olympics.

3 Speaking diaries

The teacher instructs the students in role to begin to write in their diaries (mimed). 'Speak your writing.' This can be private reflection when they do it all together, or the teacher may tap-in or create a voice collage.

4 Imaging

In this technique the individuals in the group put into words what they see in their mind's eye. The teacher uses Imaging when it is important that everyone is seeing the same place or meeting the same kind of person. Once the opening question is asked by the teacher, the picture that emerges is student-created, although the teacher is as free to contribute as the students.

The 'rule of the game' is that no contribution can be negated (unless the teacher or a student sees it as a potential problem). What emerges is cumulative and binding, although many perspectives may be described.

Two types of Imaging are shown in the following examples:

(a) Imaging the setting

Teacher: 'Big Bear has agreed to meet with us. In what kind of place do we find ourselves?'

Student 1: 'In a grassy meadow.'

Student 2: 'We are outside Big Bear's tent.'

Student 3: 'I see Big Bear standing in front of it alone.'

Student 4: 'It is hot and I can hear the sound of horses' harnesses jingling in the distance.'

Student 5: 'All the chiefs with him are wearing full war paint.' (contradicting Student 3.)

Teacher: 'And I see they are waiting to be called to the Council if Big Bear needs them.'

In building the setting, the teacher will often discover that the students will 'set in' certain ideas which she may be able to make use of in the drama work which follows. In the above example, the teacher, when in role as Big Bear, was able to introduce a new Tension when she courteously invited her captors to enter her tent. Once the picture is clear to everyone, the students and/

or teacher may want to mark out the space with a few chairs or desks.

(b)   Imaging the person
Here the student (or the teacher) acts as a blank canvas upon which the rest of the class can draw their ideas.

Teacher: 'If we are all to have an audience with Queen Isabella, what kind of person will we be meeting? Is there someone who will help us to see this person? You will not *be* her but simply allow us to get a better idea of her. (A student volunteers.) Do you think she will be sitting or standing when she first meets us?'
Student 1:   'Standing. On a platform.' (Student steps up.)
Teacher: 'As she is now?'
Student 2:   'She should be sitting.'
Student 3:   'No. Let's see if we can get her standing first.'
Student 4:   'Maybe her arms should be folded.' (Model crosses her arms over her chest.) 'No, no, I mean like this.' (He demonstrates.) 'She should look majestical.'
Teacher: 'Hmm. Yes, I can see that does give her an air of majesty.' (To the others) 'What do you think?'
Student 5:   'And her nose in the air.'
Student 6:   'She should be wearing a crown.'
Teacher: 'Have we got something that would do as a crown, or can we just imagine it?'

Sometimes young students, or even older ones, need a concrete symbol to help their commitment. In this way, students are learning about concretizing meaning, not just through language but also through symbol, which is inherently theatrical. This technique is an excellent way for the teacher to discover the kind of person the students expect to meet. She may then want to demonstrate other characteristics (consistent with the students' ideas) in order to give them opportunities to explore the problem more deeply.

Techniques which are specific to role drama

1   Making a contract
This is a significant activity which binds the students into the drama and commits them to a type of behaviour. One example is *voting* (in or out of role) to decide where to go or what to do next: 'Are we all agreed that we go with the one that has the

most votes?' Voting can be done by raising hands or ticking a choice on the blackboard. Another example is *signing your name* (in or out of role), where the student contracts to be within a group or an activity. 'Think carefully before you sign your name. There will be no going back.' A third example is *taking a vow or oath* (in role), an activity which always takes place in Ritual, and which may be verbal or written. 'Let each man now raise his right hand and swear.'

2 Releasing the end

The teacher and the students decide what the end of their drama will be: 'Will it be a successful bank robbery or will we fail?' This technique enables the teacher to build volume without the pressure from the students to find out what happens next. The following example shows how the teacher, by asking what is going to happen is giving her students the responsibility for their own drama:

> 'Do you want a waiting experience, or do you want the
> boy to become a cabbage? Or does he die? Or will there
> be a restoration to normality, realizing that "normal"
> might be different from pre-accident?' (Chapter 1, page
> 9, number 11).

3 Silence

The teacher creates a silence, a pause between what has happened and what is about to happen, to allow the students to think. For example: 'Even after the craft had disappeared, each person remained, still watching the empty sky.' . . . (silence)

4 The tangible

An object or picture is used as a focus for thought and feeling:

- 'Here is a picture of how we were.' This could be used for starting, linking or finishing.
- 'This is his sweater. Will it help you if you hold it?' The sweater has become the metaphor for the person who is no longer present.
- 'Isn't it strange that a people who can produce such beautiful things can be so cruel.'[22]

5   Demonstrating

Drama teachers do not generally show their students 'how' but demonstrating is an effective technique for helping them understand that role playing demands that they work seriously.

For example, the students are in pairs: A is Columbus and B is a newspaper reporter. The teacher says to the class, 'I'll be a newspaper reporter interviewing Bill as Columbus. You tell us if we are doing it properly.' She stops frequently to ensure that the students have a chance to contribute, to correct the procedure, and to see the possibilities and demands of the task.

6   Stranger in role

Stranger in role is the drama equivalent of bringing in the policeman when learning about the community, or inviting the drug counsellor to a health class. It is an extension of the teacher in role, where the teacher recognizes that the students need a 'new face' to respond to and where the shock value of someone new is deliberately used by the teacher to make a strong focus. The 'stranger' is someone who has not been part of the drama, but this does not mean that you are required to bring someone in off the streets! The stranger can be another member of staff, a senior student or a friend of the teacher, but he or she must be someone whom the teacher trusts and who trusts the teacher.

The teacher creates a situation:

- where the group need the stranger for his experience and/or his information, for example: apprentices meet the acknowledged expert to learn from him.
- where the group need to have their own ideas and values challenged, for example: a group of students in role as social workers have their 'charitable' plans challenged by a contented 'bag lady'.
- where the stranger needs the group to show concern for him and/or teach him something, for example: children in nursery school, playing house, are introduced by the teacher to a 'new neighbour' who needs their help because his child is sick.

Settings for the stranger in role
(a)   Naturalistic: direct, personal and informal interaction. An example is the 'new neighbour' in the nursery school.

(b)   Isolated: the initial interaction is indirect. An example is:

'What's he doing there? Look at his boots.' This talking in role or out of role can go on for some time before the 'stranger' is approached, at which time the interaction is direct and usually formal: 'Excuse me, Sir, can you tell us why you are dressed like that?'.

(c) Stranger in role as an image: statue, portrait or photograph. The interaction is indirect. For example, the students discuss among themselves what they 'read' from the image. The image can be brought to life by the students finding the key by what they do or say. The image can then reply.

A second example: In a role drama on bullfighting, the students as bullfighters in training are given the words associated with bullfighting. The teacher says, 'Not all of you will know the meaning of these words, but if you will follow me, I will show you someone who did.' The students leave the classroom. When they return the 'statue' of the matador, Belmonte, is standing on a table. 'If only you could find a way to bring the statue to life, how much he could tell you.' The students decide, after much discussion, to say in turn the words they had been given: 'fiesta, brava, corrida, honour, torero, death'. As they finish, the statue comes to life and asks the students why they are whispering those words.[23]

Preparation of the stranger in role
In preparing the 'stranger', the teacher should ensure that:

- he has sufficient information but is not overloaded.
- he can build his own role but not at the expense of the teaching objectives.
- he understands clearly that the teacher is in charge of the learning, the discipline and the drama.
- he is prepared so that he can respond to prearranged signals from the teacher.
- he understands that he is not there to put on a performance but to generate questions, language and thought, and that the less he says and does the more will be done by the students.
- he is shown how to ask in role for the teacher's help if he needs it.

Natural good manners should be shown to the stranger, whatever the role being represented. If this special convention breaks down it is the teacher's job to protect the stranger. It is also the teacher's job to keep the focus on the stranger:

'Why is he looking so tired, I wonder?' (expression)
'The dress is old, but the bonnet appears to be new.' (costume)
'What do you think he has written on his scroll?' (props)

Stranger in role is a very effective technique which requires good preparation. However, there is no point in the teacher using it if she can achieve her objectives better by taking the role herself.

Questions

You will have noticed that many of the techniques suggested here are introduced through questions. Although we have spent a whole chapter on questioning, we want to remind you here about the technique of questioning. Questions can be asked in or out of role, at the plot, meaning or feeling level.

Teacher questioning out of role
- At the plot level: 'Should we all bow together or should we approach the King separately?'
- At the meaning level: 'Is there something in the room which would help us to believe that he is the King?'
- At the feeling level: 'Was there any time when you were not comfortable?'

Teacher questioning in role
- At the plot level: 'Are we all ready for take-off? Signals, do you have contact? Power, do you have contact? Engines, what are your read-outs?'
- At the meaning level: 'Shall we all switch over from earth-receiving to satellite-receiving now?'
- At the feeling level: 'Have you a last message to relay?'

Instruction

Instruction is a perfectly valid, healthy technique to use in a drama class. It is used to move the students quickly into the next activity. The teacher must know what and how she is going to instruct. Much time is wasted when the teacher says, 'I wonder if you would like to get into groups of five . . . no, six . . . no . . . How many are we? . . . Mary's away? . . . Will she be here later?' She should say, 'Three groups of five and one of six.'

Instruction is minimal language, delivered so that all may hear. It can be used in role and the same criteria apply: 'Stand in your family groups. The authorities will be here presently.'

Although instruction dictates what is to be done, it need not be regarded as unchangeable. Students will often ask if they can work in a different way. If the learning objectives (see Chapter 6, page 164, The Play for the Teacher) will not be altered drastically, and if the administration is manageable, there is no reason why the teacher should not be flexible. This is shown by the following examples:

Focus: to explore, using one's own story as a source for role.
Instruction: A is the listener. B will tell his own story to A as if B were his own mother or father.
Student: 'I think I could do it better if I could be A's boyfriend.'
Teacher: 'Good. Have a try.'

Focus: to explore, taking on the role of someone familiar but much older.
Instruction: as above.
Student: 'I think I could do it better if I could be A's boyfriend.'
Teacher: 'No. I'm sorry but it's important that you work in this exercise as one of your parents.'

Side coaching

This is a facilitating technique in exercise or improvisation where the teacher is outside the work in progress, making suggestions which the students may incorporate into their work. The teacher's voice is quiet. Side coaching is a non-disruptive technique which relies on the teacher working alongside the students, as shown in the following example:

Correcting: 'She's still not listening to you. Find another way to get her attention.'
Suggesting: 'It may be easier if you don't crowd her.'
Challenging: 'Come on, Sarah, you can find something to interest her.'

Facilitating group work

When the students are working in groups, the teacher often feels she has no part to play and isolates herself. What she should do is use this time to:

- check that each group understands the task and is at work on it. 'Are you having a problem? Is this not clear?'
- check that the social health of the group is being maintained. 'What's happened to George's idea?'
- observe the content of the work in order to check that it is congruent with the ideas and events already known. 'But you decided how many there were and what they stood for. Are ten not enough to do the job?'
- keep a time check. 'Will you need more time?'
- offer suggestions if it is appropriate. (Generally only when asked.) 'Have you thought of . . .?'
- operate as 'carrier pigeon'. 'A couple of groups want to use a riser. Would that be helpful to you?'
- sense when to interrupt the work in order to restructure, clarify, suggest or share ideas with the whole class.
- provide an opportunity for a fast-working group to slow down and examine their work. This must not be 'busy work' but an opportunity for them to deepen their understanding. 'Let's see what you've got. . . . That's coming! Now you will have a chance to work on that interesting relationship you've set up.'
- sense when it would be more productive to enter a group in role, often using a fringe role.
- observe the over-all tone of the class.

Private instruction

This technique is used in improvisation or role drama when it is important for some to have information which the others do not have. The teacher withdraws the students and gives them information which they then use to change the texture of the work. Here are two examples:

Improvisation in groups
The fathers are withdrawn and told that they have lost their jobs but must keep this news from the family who are discussing a holiday.

Role drama
'Can I have two guides from the tribe to come with me to protect your interests?' The teacher leaves the room with the two students. She returns with them in role as before. 'I have returned as I promised you. Here are your friends, safe.' After

she 'leaves', the group question the guides. They say nothing because their tongues have been 'cut out'. (David Booth, Workshop, November 1984.)

Questioning groups in a fringe role

Students have no difficulty in accepting a teacher in a fringe role, that is, the one who has the right to ask questions and who listens to the answers with consideration. We have described this technique when the teacher is working in role in a role drama, but it is also a means of sharing the work of groups improvising on the same source.

Teacher: 'I understand you have a concern, Captain Smith?'
Student: 'We don't feel we were properly prepared for the mission.'
Teacher (commenting):
     'You don't, then, see much hope for success?' (She moves to next group.)
Teacher: 'Who is the captain here? There seems to be some question of the value of this mission. What are your feelings about this, Captain Robinson?'

The teacher talks to members of other groups in this way, weaving their responses together so that many facets of the experience are revealed. This helps to build meaning for each participant and a collective meaning for the group.

Non-evaluative feedback

In Sharing, Showing and Demonstration, applause should be discouraged and the teacher must make this clear right from the start. Work at the explorative level is inhibited if value judgements are made because the students assess their work on the length and strength of the clapping (which is often merely an indication of the popularity of the players!). At the same time, the teacher must respond to the work, although in a non-judgemental way:

'This is what I saw. Is this what you wanted me to see?'
'This is what I heard. Is this what you wanted me to hear?'
'What could you have done differently?'
'If you had more time, which bit would you work on?'

Conclusion

There are, of course, very many techniques. The more you read, observe others teaching and teach drama yourself, the wider your repertoire of techniques will become. When you instinctively do something in your teaching that really helps your students in their work (or they suggest something), be sure to write it down. There is nothing more frustrating than using the same material again and not being able to remember what you did, but only that it was terrific the last time. Be aware, too, that you will have your favourite strategies and techniques, but, like any good recipe, over-use dulls the taste buds as it will your students' responses. There is nothing that inhibits learning more than your students thinking 'Oh, no. Here we go again!'

Skill-building exercises for teachers
1   Read!
2   Observe!
3   Practise!

References
1   Goffman, Erving, *1961 Encounters: Two Studies in the Sociology of Interaction*, Bobs Merrill, Indianapolis, 1962
2   Stewig, John, *Spontaneous Drama, a Language Art*, pp 3–4
3   Bolton, Gavin, *Towards a Theory of Drama in Education*, p 119, Longman, 1979
4   Saint-Denis, Michel, *Training for the Theatre*, p 111, Theatre Arts Books, New York, 1982
5   O'Neill, Cecily and Lambert, Alan, *Drama Structures*, 'The Way West', p 37, Hutchinson, London, 1982
6   DuMaurier, Daphne, *Rebecca*, Victor Gollancz Ltd, London 1938
7   O'Neill, Cecily and Lambert, Alan, *Drama Structures*, p 28, Hutchinson, London, 1982
8   Saint-Denis, Michel, *Training for the Theatre*, Suria Saint-Denis ed., Theatre Arts Books, New York, 1982
9   Davis, David, 'Gavin Bolton interviewed by David Davis', p 7, *2D*, vol. 4, no. 2, Spring 1985
10 Lundy and Booth, *Interpretation*, p 73, Academic Press Canada, 1983
11 Rothenberg, Jerome, ed., *Technicians of the Sacred*, Doubleday Anchor Book, 1969
12 Julian, Nancy, R., 'Miss Pickett's Secret', *Brown is the Back of a*

    Toad, Colours, a language arts program, p 69, Longmans Canada
    Ltd., 1974
13 Heathcote, Dorothy, *General Introduction*, University of
    Newcastle upon Tyne, Institute of Education (undated)
14 O'Neill, Cecily and Lambert, Alan, *Drama Structures*, p 115,
    Hutchinson, 1982
15 O'Neill, Cecily and Lambert, Alan, *Drama Structures*, pp 77
    and 79, Hutchinson, 1982
16 Koppel, Tina, 'What is meant by drama in depth?', *FINE
    Journal*, Alberta, 1983
17 *Three Looms Waiting*, BBC TV, 1971. 'Jezebel' is the second
    example in the film, Tom Stabler is the teacher
18 Morgan and Saxton, 'Structures, Strategies, Techniques',
    CCYDA Winter Journal, 1983
19 Gavin Bolton interviewed by David Davis, *2D*, vol. 4, no. 2,
    Spring 1985
20 Linnell, Rosemary, *Approaching Classroom Drama*, pp 60, 61
21 Wagner, B. J., *Dorothy Heathcote: Drama as a Learning Medium*,
    p 76
22 Fines, John, 'Teaching strategies, looking at history', *Drama
    and the Whole Curriculum*, pp 120, 121
23 Tarlington, C., Verriour, P., *Offstage*, pp 156, 157

6

Planning

The creator needs problems
The problem is an unlearned skill
In solving problems, the creator learns skills
He uses his skills to turn new problems
Into new skills

When we work we have only problems and skills
Respect the problem!
Do not turn back when you see it
Or turn aside
It holds the secret of change
In it is hidden the new skill

Look at the problem closely
Understand it has many sides
But fewer solutions
Before the solutions are known you must know the sides
This is the law of nature[1]

Risk brings its own rewards: the exhilaration of breaking
through, of getting to the other side, the relief of a conflict
healed, the clarity when a paradox dissolves. Eventually
we know deeply that the other side of every fear is a
freedom.[2]

In the last decade a great number of books on educational drama
have been published. There is now a fine collection of descriptions of drama lessons in which the teacher is no longer merely
instructing or directing, but is, part of the time, inside the drama
in role, discovering, questioning and problem-solving with her
students. These descriptions do not simply illustrate teaching
points but stand as examples for teaching analysis and plans

for lessons. It is no longer necessary for teachers to invent each lesson or lesson unit, with the attendant anxieties of: Will it work? Have I started in the right way? Is it too easy or too hard for them? Would I be safer out of role? They can turn to books such as *Drama Structures* (O'Neill and Lambert), *Offstage* (Tarlington and Verriour) and *Drama Guidelines* (O'Neill, Lambert, Linnell and Warr-Wood) and find excellent, tested drama lessons which will allow them to start off with confidence.

Any teacher, however inexperienced, will realize that there comes a point in the lesson when the students do not give the answer which is described in the sample lesson. This moment is the one to which the drama teacher should look forward, for it is 'the moment of risk' when the students begin to take over responsibility for the direction of their work. For some teachers, however, it is 'the point of anxiety' which manifests itself in one of two ways: the teacher 'freezes' because her pattern of expectation has been shattered or she spends the next few minutes (or the rest of the lesson) manipulating the students' answers and suggestions back into the format of the sample lesson.

The contextual structure for drama planning

In an attempt to release the teacher from the restrictions of the contextual descriptions of sample drama lessons, we analyzed examples in order to try to 'peel back' the layers of story and plot and reveal a framework which would act as a guide to planning, a support at 'the point of anxiety' and a basis for evaluation. We have called this framework 'A Contextual Structure for Drama Planning'. (See table on next page.)

Substructure

'Unless account is taken by the teacher of what drives her and also of what drives the class to choose the ways that they do, the drama will inevitably lose a sense of direction.'[3]

A Contextual Structure for Drama Planning

When creating a structure, one starts with the foundation. Please read from the bottom (number 1, Initial considerations) through to the top (number 7, The Play for Them).

Superstructure: what is seen/observed

7 *The Play for Them:* how the students see their work

Structure: what is planned

4 *Focus:*	5 *Strategy:*	5 *Activity:*	5 *Techniques:*	6 *Administration:*
What is the problem (i.e. the particular idea dictated by the source) to be explored?	The means by which the focus will be explored, i.e. exercise, Mantle of the Expert, depiction, etc.	What the students will do.	What devices does the teacher use to implement the strategy? i.e. in role, side-coaching, instruction, etc.	How does the teacher help the students to carry out the activity? i.e. groupings, space, materials, etc.

Substructure: what lies underneath

3 *Taxonomy expectations*: What degrees of personal engagement can be expected/are needed.

The Play for The Teacher:
The teacher's educational objectives.

2 *Learning considerations*
Students' Personal Luggage:
What is brought into the classroom – knowledge, feelings, values, understandings and experiences from inside and outside the school.

1 *Initial considerations*

Content: (a) from the curriculum i.e. history, maths, English, etc.
(b) from the students' suggestions i.e. 'What do you want to make a play about?'
(c) from class needs i.e: non-subject life learning (Bolton, 1982)

The Social Health of the Class:
The group dynamic, influenced by the position of the class in relation to the school and the community, and by the way in which they view each other.

Teacher's Personal Luggage:
What is brought into the classroom – education (general and specialized), feelings, values, understandings and experiences.

Initial considerations (Substructure)

Teacher's Personal Luggage
A good drama teacher is well-read, not simply professionally (through an interest in drama books, journals and articles) but also because she is supported by a wide exposure to great literature. The latter should include, as well as her own preferences, novels, stories for children and young adults, myths, legends, fairy and folk tales, 'bible stories' of all religions, and the history of mankind with its heroes and villains. It is also important that she maintains contact with current writing, TV, films, plays, art, music, newspapers, comic books, periodicals, exhibitions and museum displays, so that she is up-to-date with the world and the community as well as the school. This background, though desirable for all teachers, is a practical necessity for teachers of drama because it is the source of classroom ideas.

In spite of being so knowledgeable, the paradox is that a good drama teacher does not have to have all the answers. She must accept the fact that some students will know and have experienced a great deal more than she has in some areas. (*We* know far less than our students about space and computers, we know nothing of what it is like to be the child of divorced parents and we know only vicariously what it is like to be without warm clothing in the winter.)

For a teacher to accept her own ignorance and lack of experience is to put herself in a very exposed position. She will have to say 'I don't know' and 'What do you think we should do next?' – each a step into the unknown. She can only step into the unknown if she knows what she is carrying with her. She must understand the principles and standards by which she conducts her life and she must ensure that her students are aware, from the beginning of the year, of the standards that are important to her. For example, 'Good work, to me, is high quality endeavour. I'd rather see you set your sights high, work hard and fail, than mess about with poor quality work.' She must know what it is she values.

● Are you, for instance, prepared to handle 'Teenagers and Drugs', as requested by a class of nine-year-olds? Do you feel that children of this age shouldn't know about such things? Have you chosen to teach in elementary school because you hoped to avoid both teenagers and drugs? Are you worried about administration and parental reaction? About the topic?

About your position? Do you think that kids that age won't know enough? Or are you worried because they might know things which you feel you cannot handle?
- Are you prepared to use *your* values in order to stimulate students to identify *theirs*, as did the teacher whose questions to herself you have just read?
- Are you prepared to work in a situation which runs counter to your own value system, so that students may explore the implications of their action when they follow their own value system? A group of ten-year-olds chooses to do a 'bank robbery'. Will you go along in order to show them the responsibility of living outside the law? (See Chapter 1, pages 13 to 16.)
- Are you prepared to set aside your personal values in order for students to express theirs? For example, you believe that it is more important to be at home with your children in their early years than to work outside the home. Your students want to make a docudrama on a woman's right to fulfil herself through a career. Or you think monsters are bad for children. Will you allow six-year-olds, who want to do a drama about the Incredible Hulk, to learn about fear by frightening themselves?
- Have you the courage to say 'No' when you are not prepared to explore a subject with them? It is better to do this than to lose their respect by pretending to deal with it.
- Are you prepared, at the appropriate time, to share your values? For example, 'I cannot make a hero out of someone who is dishonest.'
- Are you prepared to admit to your students that you have made a mistake? You would be surprised how understanding they can be if you let them discover that you, too, are human! For example, 'I talked too much!', 'This isn't working the way I think it should!', 'I've made a terrible mistake!'

Concomitant with principles and standards are the teacher's 'teaching thresholds'. According to Heathcote they are:

- Decision-taking
- Noise
- Distance
- Size of groups
- Teaching registers (teaching role)
- Status of the teacher[4]

These thresholds are the 'conditions' by which the teacher conducts her class and her relationship with the students. For example:

- At what point is she prepared to let the students take responsibility and what decisions must she keep in her own hands to fulfil her objectives?
- How much noise can she work in without being distressed?
- Does she accept physical contact?
- Does working in whole group make her feel she has lost control?
- In what role is she most comfortable (see Chapter 3)?
- How does she want to be seen by her colleagues and her students?

At the same time, she must consider:

- Are these conditions productive for her students and for her colleagues? (Are her students more comfortable with a teacher than a buddy? Is her creative noise driving the French teacher crazy?)
- Is she prepared to cross these thresholds in order to develop a more flexible teaching repertoire? This does not mean that she has to jump in the deep end (she may drown and take her students with her!) but she can plan a lesson which will include a few minutes of threshold crossing from which she can step back gracefully.

  'At the centre of all we do in schools and in drama class is ourselves. We must never forget that, as teachers, we are there for more than just the service of our students. Our needs are also struggling to be met in our school relationship and to pretend otherwise would be to overlook a vital ingredient in planning.'[5]

Social health of the class
The other centre of teaching is, of course, the class. Successful planning is dependent upon the teacher considering the social health of the class with which she is working. She must consider outside influences:

- From what kind of community do the students come: urban, rural, racially mixed?

- How interested are the parents in their children's education?
- How stable is the population?

She must consider school influences:

- Are they at the bottom of the school, in the middle, at the top?
- Are they mainstream, special, or mixed?
- Is the school administration supportive of drama?
- What is the reputation of drama in the school?

She must consider the group dynamic:

- Are they a cohesive whole, are there warring factions, or is the situation somewhere in between?
- Do they have other classes together?
- Are there leaders? What does their leadership represent? (Leadership through bullying, popularity, by natural talent?)
- To what extent can they agree on the 'rules of the game' and play by them?
- To what extent can they accept the imaginative world and play in it?

Outside influences and school influences tend to be constant throughout the school year, but one of the teacher's overall objectives can be either to improve the group dynamic of the class or, if it is already sound, to recognize it as a signal that they are ready for more challenging work. As the social health of the class improves, they will be able to take on more and more responsibility for their own learning. It is as unproductive to expect too little of the students as it is to force them into situations for which they are unprepared socially.

Content (What is to be taught)
Whether drama is subject or method, the material will come from the curriculum, from the students' wants or from the teacher's observation of the needs of the class. The curriculum will tell you what to teach but not how to teach it, because designers of curricula, being teachers themselves, understand that learning depends upon successful interaction between student and teacher and that there are many 'roads to Rome'. The following are examples:

Drama as subject
The drama teacher will teach Improvisation

- because it is the next unit in the curriculum and the students are ready for it.
- the students have seen Theatre Sports at the International Children's Festival and see this activity as 'real' theatre. The teacher recognizes that nothing further will be accomplished until this 'want' is satisfied. The teacher's objective now becomes 'What learning can be promoted?' (The Play for the Teacher).
- In order for the work in role drama to have more meaning, the teacher perceives that the students need to have more background and sets them into improvisation to build volume (see Chapter 1, page 10, number 16, and page 13, number 2).

Drama as method
The classroom teacher using drama as method can employ drama

- to explore the human dilemma in History;[6] to clarify the students' understanding in literature;[7] to personalize research in science (see page 62)
- A class of eight-year-olds have seen a cartoon of the Pied Piper and want to be the rats. A dance drama culminating in a procession following the Pied Piper satisfies them. At the same time, it meets the teacher's objective to have the students cooperate as a whole group, prior to working in a role drama (The Play for the Teacher).
- A class of twelve-year-old learning disabled children desperately need opportunities to express themselves in writing. The teacher uses a role drama about 'Big Rigs' as a stimulus for many kinds of writing.

Learning considerations (Substructure)

The Play for the Teacher

This term, originated by Geoff Gillam in 1974, is an accurate and appropriate description of the particular learning which the drama teacher hopes for. It is generally used to replace 'educational objectives'. In sports it is known as 'the game plan'. The teacher considers:

- skills that can be practised

- skills that can be developed
- social skills that can be exercised
- social skills that can be developed
- understandings that can be employed in a new situation
- learning that can be tested in a different situation
- meanings that can be explored.

The teacher does not necessarily reveal her 'play' to the students as this tends to prohibit, rather than promote, learning. However, it must be carefully thought out, because it is the 'why' of what is to be done and is her basis for evaluation and assessment.

Students' Personal Luggage
This represents the individual contribution (negative or positive) that each member of the class makes. Personal Luggage includes:

- knowledge of the subject
- general knowledge
- skills
- health
- values
- experiences
- feelings.

Successful teaching and learning is dependent upon the teacher's awareness that each student has a personal life which will have an effect upon his work and his relationships, and that every day it will be different. You cannot put all your eggs in the basket of yesterday's splendid work but, equally, you must be well-planned in order to accommodate new behaviour and energy.

- George, who yesterday was a firm, calm and logical Pied Piper, arrives late for class and is obviously angry about something.
- The class has been kept in at break because no-one will own up to the broken window.
- Everyone is either getting the 'flu, has the 'flu, or is getting over the 'flu (and so are you!)

These are but three of an infinite number of variables which make teaching so challenging. It is equally true that yesterday's suet dumplings can float in today as chocolate mousse! So you must be prepared.

Taxonomy expectations

To complete the Substructure, the teacher must consider the Taxonomy, using it as a guide to the levels of engagement that she can expect or that she needs from her students for a successful lesson.

If you remember (page 28), the Taxonomy is cumulative, so the first task is to get all the students interested. For example when improvising, the teacher may start

- with a game involving improvisation skills, for example changing object game, or
- 'Today we are developing an essential theatrical skill which even Laurence Olivier found difficult. Let's see how we get on.'

Interest may be all you will get or need in the first lesson, for if you have chosen the wrong game you will need to substitute another, and if the game generates excitement leading to discussion and suggestions from the students to do it differently, you will need to take the time to let them direct their own learning. (Note that they are engaged in the game but not yet in Improvisation.)

The next strategy will be to find the means of engaging in Improvisation. As students become more involved, the teacher plans activities where Commitment and Internalization can take place, and Interpreting may follow if it is appropriate or part of The Play for the Teacher.

Thus the Taxonomy acts

- as a point of reference which dictates the complexity at which the teacher expects the students to work
- as a means of assessing the progress of the work, and
- in conjunction with The Play for the Teacher, as a guide to the quality of the students' work.

Conclusions

In grappling with what is to be taught (Content), the teacher must be wise to her own Personal Luggage and the Social Health of the class. She must be aware of the changing nature of the Students' Personal Luggage; she must determine her educational objectives and know how to move through the Taxonomy.

Let us look at two examples of Substructuring; the first where the material has been dictated by the Curriculum Guide (Drama as Subject) and the second where the teacher uses drama as a way of teaching in the general curriculum (Drama as Method).

Example 1
The Curriculum Guide states that one unit will be on Improvisation (Content)
Substructure:

- The teacher works equally well with small or large groups (Teacher's Personal Luggage)
- Her students can work responsibly in pairs (Social Health)
- Their previous drama work has tended to be shallow (Students' Personal Luggage)
- The teacher wants some honest work and to have the class work as a whole group (The Play for the Teacher)
- The teacher looks for an activity which starts from where they are but where the task is challenging enough to intrigue them (Taxonomy 1) and one that will allow her opportunities for intervention so that she may monitor closely the quality of the work (The Play for the Teacher)

The following three steps outline the teacher's thinking about the activity at this stage and do not represent a lesson plan.

Step 1: 'Choose a gift for your partner.'
Step 2: 'Present this gift to your partner who will know from what you say and how you say it and the way in which it is presented, what you are giving him.
Step 3: 'The receiver will return the gift in such a way that it does not offend the giver.'

Example 2
A teacher of 10, 11 and 12-year-old 'slow learners' decides to use drama as a stimulus for written work (Content).
Substructure:

- The teacher is confident working with large groups in drama (Teacher's Personal Luggage)
- The students are active, aggressive and need constant supervision (Social Health)
- The students do not enjoy written work, their compositions are dull and grammatically inept, and their writing is always

accompanied by sighs and groans! (Students' Personal Luggage)
- The teacher wants the class to work individually on a piece of descriptive writing (The Play for the Teacher)
- The school is on a main road. The teacher has noticed at break that her students spend a lot of time at the fence, noting the 'Big Rigs' as they thunder by (Students' Personal Luggage). Her first move in the role drama is to welcome them in role as designers of 'Big Rig' trucks (Taxonomy 1).

During this unit the students are involved in listing special features of the trucks, writing critiques of their performances, writing memos suggesting improvements, creating advertising copy and writing promotional folders.

Superstructure

The Play for Them

Although it would seem logical to look at Structure, it is the Superstructure which must concern us next. How the students see their work (The Play for Them) is an important consideration in planning. It helps you to prepare, not so much what you are teaching, but how you will teach it. Students should be able to say what they were doing in their drama class and to do so with the correct vocabulary. There is no reason why even very young students should not be able to tell their friends, parents or other teachers what was going on in their drama work. A good lesson should 'demystify' the proceedings and your students' ability to describe their activities clearly will also help to validate the subject to your colleagues.

> 'What did you do in drama today?'
> 'Oh, I dunno, but I had a really good time. I like doing drama, it's so much fun!'

This is hardly what you want the Principal to hear, however earnest and well-intentioned its expression!

If the students can encapsulate their view of the experience in such a way that it describes some aspect of the lesson, then it is possible that learning has taken place.

> 'Rick came home from kindergarten today and told me with great excitement what had happened at school.

Instead of the usual "nothing much" he said, "We
helped the teacher who was the King to solve this   .
problem of a dinosaur which was sitting on his bridge".'
                              Letter from a parent to a teacher

The teacher's planning, therefore, must include her mental
forecast of how the students might perceive the work. This
projection will help her to clarify and refine her plan.
     We have now arrived at 'the moment of risk'. What happens
next will be tested in the classroom.

Structure

What is planned

How does the drama teacher learn to think of risk, not as synony-
mous with failure but as an agent of success? The first thing to
remember is Dorothy Heathcote's admonition:

'You can't get away with shabby planning, ever!'

But remember also that, as time goes by, hard labour becomes
the craft and the craft becomes the art. If you drive a car, think
of all the things you keep in mind: speed, signalling, gearing,
steering, looking ahead, keeping your eye on the rear-view
mirror, seeing the other cars, watching out for pedestrians,
adjusting to the conditions of the road, the weather, the volume
of traffic, *and* carrying on a conversation and twiddling the dial
to find some nice music! None of this is difficult when you are
used to it because you know where your concentration is most
needed. It is the same in drama. We can assure you that careful
planning pays off in the end. Planning provides the invisible
safety net when you appear to be working without one.
     The Structure is made up of five parts which act as guides
to the teacher's planning and as reference points in the actual
operation of the lesson:

Dramatic Focus: What is to be explored.
Strategy: The frame through which the students will be taken into
action, and the means by which they will explore the focus.
Activity: The strategy in action, or what the students will do.
Techniques: The devices which the teacher uses to implement the
strategy.

Administration: What is needed to assist the teacher and students to carry out the activity.

The teacher's ability to keep these five points in mind during the class gives her the flexibility to change, adapt and reinforce any part of the lesson, for planning does not just take place before lessons and between lessons but also during them when you are 'on your feet'.

There are many books with ideas for dramatic activities and it is not the purpose of this book to add to them. The functions and some operations of Strategies and Techniques have already been described in Chapter 5. Dramatic Focus and Administration are the only parts of the Structure which need to be examined here.

Dramatic Focus

Every single lesson is part of a unit and every unit is part of a wider educational context which will have its own particular focus. The Educational Context refers to the subject being taught. The Educational Focus represents the particular material, skills or area of exploration of the subject. The Dramatic Context is a brief synthesis of the unit of drama work to be undertaken. The Dramatic Focus of each lesson represents the specific 'lens' through which the students will explore the Dramatic Context and it is the means through which the teacher will endeavour to achieve some parts of her Educational Focus. The Activity will be chosen as the most appropriate action by which the students will explore the Dramatic Focus.

For example:
Educational Context: History (17-year-olds)[8]
Educational Focus: The causes of the Second World War
Dramatic Context: An exploration through Improvisation of the implications of taking and holding power.
Dramatic Focus: To explore the 'look' of power
Strategy: Craft
Activity: Building a 'great throne'
Technique: Instruction: 'Use whatever is in the room'
Administration: Whole class, some large pieces of material, props box available; Time: 10 minutes

or
Educational Context: Drama

Educational Focus: Small group dynamics, listening skills
Dramatic Context: Creating and sharing a sound poem
Dramatic Focus: To explore non-verbal sounds
Strategy: Sound exercises (non-verbal)
Activity: Murray Schafer's pictographs[9]
Technique: Instruction, side-coaching, demonstration?
Administration: Five groups of four, 20 copies of pictograph sheet.

The Dramatic Focus is the keystone around which each particular lesson plan is built. Teachers tend to plan through activities: 'What are the students going to *do*?', instead of considering first what needs to be explored and second what activity is most appropriate for the exploration. For example:

Teacher A: 'I will get the students to do 'Mirrors' tomorrow and for the last ten minutes they can play a game, "Keeper of the Keys".'

Teacher B: 'My students need to explore communication with a partner without words. I can use mirrors, movement, or silent improvisations.'

If Mirrors do not work for Teacher A she can draw another activity out of her compendium but, as she had no Dramatic Focus, she has no guide to help her selection. Students are always aware when the teacher is working off the top of her head and will view the lesson as 'busy work'.

If Mirrors do work for Teacher A and she does not know what her Focus is, she has no guide for her questions, side-coaching or extensions, and, again, the students will be aware of a lack of direction. If the teacher does not know 'why', the students certainly won't!

Teacher B, on the other hand, has other appropriate activities at her disposal should her first choice prove unsuitable. If her first choice is working well, then she will know what questions to ask, what comments to make and what additional techniques she can use to extend the work because she knows why she is doing what she is doing. We have never seen a dramatic activity work well where the teacher cannot identify her Focus.

Administration
Administration is often ignored by inexperienced teachers. It may be the last part of the Structure but it is not the least important. Any teacher who has no pencils or paper available at the moment of reflection in the drama, where the students are to write in

role, will lose that for which she and her students have been working.

Administration is not only concerned with props, it is also concerned with:

- arranging for the space (library? gym?)
- arrangement of space (desks against the wall)
- what school activities might interfere (school dentist, sports match)
- what letters need to be written (to the parents? to outside sources?)
- which teachers need to be informed (the librarian? the deputy headmaster?)
- what reference books, pictures, films, records are to be used?
- what equipment has to be ordered (projector, record player?)
- what photocopying needs to be done? How many copies?
- what size groups are needed?
- what time limits are needed for the activities?

To ignore any of the parts of the Structure in planning could be compared to doing *Anne of Green Gables* in Thunder Bay, when props, costumes and sets are in a railway siding in Espanola and the orchestra is on its way to Tuktoyaktuk in the North West Territories!

Bringing it all together

Let us now attempt to bring all three parts of the Contextual Structure together in a demonstration of 'how it works'. (We are indebted to Betty Mundy for this idea, which she used with her students at Princess Elizabeth Elementary School, Welland, Ontario, 1985.)

Substructure: see page 168, Example 2
Number in class: 18 (14 boys, 4 girls)
Place: Classroom
Time: 10.00 to 10.45 am
Educational Context: Language Arts
Dramatic Context: Designing and promotion of 'Big Rigs' in a role drama
Superstructure: 'The makers of "Big Rigs" want our ideas on new safety features. We have to work professionally.'
Teacher preparation: Write away for Big Rig posters, promotional

folders, blueprints. Write to the Automobile Association for truck drivers' 'rules of the road'.

Pre-drama: Prepare classroom the night before, put up posters, arrange display, create design corner with wood pieces, glue, rulers, hammers, paint.

Day 1 (Play for the Teacher)

Informal, simply to introduce the material. Use the surprise of the material to stimulate the children to share their interest with one another and to see what information they already have. (See table on next page.)

Stage One: Assessment (Teacher's Journal)

Interest: All interested and most engaged. Mary and Jane a bit puzzled.

Copying skills: Penmanship still terrible, but spelling is accurate for the most part. (Peter still reversing 'th') and work laid out surprisingly professionally – the blueprints helped.

Imaginative skills: Lots of contributions to the drama in ideas, and Mantle of Expert well-maintained for the most part. Probably half were still themselves, but George is ready to run the design department! Alison not well, see the psychologist about Jamie. Andrew mentioned 'we all talked like big people' and we had a good discussion about 'how you talk and what you do helps to make the drama better' – nice evaluation from them.

Notes: Had to drive them out at break. Much boasting, and I heard Mary (!) tell Lissie Mayberry after lunch that she couldn't play hopscotch as she had 'business' to attend to in the classroom. (Superstructure – how Mary sees the play for Her.) Found her working on her sketch. They were worried at the end of the day about the safety of their designs. (Possible spy? Look up the Iacocca biography, it could be a useful tension.) How much responsibility can I release to George? He and Ann are to talk to their dads.

When planning, each lesson, even if it is one of a series, should have the same structure as the well-made play. Although the example you have just read does not have the same dramatic power as the Bolton lesson on Improvisation in Chapter 1 (see page 7), it does follow the structure of Exposition, Rising Action and Denouement. For these students, however, the excitement of working in a context of which they had never thought they could be a part and to which they realized they could contribute, was enough to sustain a sense of the collective and to demand

Drama Day 1

Dramatic Focus	Strategy	Activity	Technique	Administration
To explore what it is like to have the responsibility for designing the special safety features of the Big Rigs	Mantle of the Expert	1. Listening	Teacher in role as administrator (not designer!) Mid-high status.	Tables in a semi-circle, felt pens, newsprint, blueprints standing by.
		Introduce self, put students into Mantle of the Expert, problem: safety features. Tension: to come up with designs that will sell; possible within 5 days?		
		2. In role begin to sketch out suggestions.	Side coaching, building volume. Remind students about competition, professional work, innovative ideas.	ditto
		3. Discussion: 'Perhaps it would be a good time to share our ideas and concerns about the project.'	List special features on board (their ideas).	
		Copy from the board onto sketches (Play for the Teacher)		Chalk.

Possible conclusion: 'Do you think that by tomorrow you will have enough ideas to begin your models?' 'Should we write down any questions for Ann and George to ask their fathers?' (who drive 'Big Rigs')

a high (for them) degree of engagement (Taxonomy). The opportunity for synthesizing their ideas on the board and then recording them on their individual 'blueprints', resulted in an aggressive approach to the task, rather than, as before, to each other. Certainly at the end of the lesson there was a feeling of satisfaction on the part of the participants and on the part of the teacher as she saw the initial success of her learning objectives (The Play for the Teacher).

A first lesson is all very well and good, but what happens next? And the day after that? Having got off the ground, where does the work go from there?

In her planning for Day 2, the Substructure and the Superstructure remain the same, but looking at her Assessment the teacher knows that she must include hearing from Ann and George and making the models. (See table on next page.)

Dramathink or how to take the source apart

Look back at the driving analogy on page 169 in this chapter. What we described was the *act* of driving, but what was left out was *why* you had got into your car in the first place.

When you are planning a car trip you sit down with the atlas and the road book and all those exciting little pamphlets which tell you about the places you will or can pass through and what there is to see. You then plot a tour which will include all the things you might want to do. If a place is interesting you may want to stay there, if it is not, you know you can move on. If there is an interesting side road, there is no reason not to take it if it seems to be another way to the same destination. If you know why you are taking this journey and what you want to get out of it (Substructure and Superstructure), each day's travel can be planned as it arrives. The plan itself can be changed if you have to make a detour or someone you meet suggests you see something you had not considered. The way a drama teacher thinks about the Content is much the same. Having selected the material, the teacher needs to take it apart in order to see its potential and which pieces will yield the learning she requires.

Of all the operations that a drama teacher undertakes the one that appears to be the most difficult is *how* do drama teachers think. The most frequently heard remark at any teaching demonstration has always been, 'Yes, but how did she *know* what to do/say?'

Dorothy Heathcote did a workshop with teachers on this

Drama Day 2

Dramatic Focus	Strategy	Activity	Technique	Administration
To translate the sketch to the model.	Mantle of the Expert.	1. Listen to Ann and George reporting.	Can they do this in role?	As in Day 1. Check craft corner.
		2. To make models.	Use pressure of 5 days. Side coach in role.	Move to craft corner.
	Questions	3. Discussion. How are you getting on? What problems? What concerns?	Teacher in role.	Return to 'meeting room'.

Possible conclusions: 'You can work on your models if you finish your work early.'

very matter. She asked groups of three to find out how quickly
they could move the talking into action. A was to ask the question
'What do you want to make a play about?'. B was to reply and
C was to record the negotiation. After the question was asked in
one group, the answer B gave was 'Romans!' After agonized
minutes had gone by and A was still trying to find the way into
action, Dorothy came by. The situation was described to her and
she said, 'What do you want to make a play about?' 'The
Romans.' She leant forward, gently grasping the upper arm of B
and said 'You must have been a very strong man. How long
have you been imprisoned here under the Coliseum?' She and
B were immediately engaged in a dramatic predicament. Unfortu-
nately, no students of ours ever said that they wanted to make
a play about the Romans and so, although we knew how to
handle that situation should it ever arise, we still didn't know
how Dorothy had 'got there' even though we could see that it
was the natural and obvious thing to do *after* she had done it!
At that time even Dorothy could not describe how she thought
of that action and we put it down to genius, magic or charisma,
none of which definitions made it any more possible that the
magic would happen for us.

Since that time, a wealth of writings on educational drama
and exchanges of master teachers of international reputation have
provided the classroom teacher with experiences and theory
upon which analysis can be based. Each of the models of thinking
which follow serve not only for finding a way to start but as a
means of spreading out all the ideas so they can be looked at.
The teacher then has a compendium of ideas, themes, resources,
activities, roles, questions and possibilities to which she can
return at any time during, or between, ensuing lessons. Although
each teacher has one or two models with which she is particularly
comfortable, we have found that each model has something to
offer and that the material will often dictate the most suitable
approach.

Models of thinking

1 Thematic Networking (Bolton, *ABCDE Journal*, Spring, 1983)
2 Categorizing (based on Edward Hall, 1959, adopted by
   Heathcote, adapted by Morgan)
3 The Brotherhoods (Heathcote, 1976)
4 Man vs. Man, Nature, Gods (Heathcote, 1976)
5 The Reverse (based on Brian Way, 1967)

6   The Unanswered Question (Morgan, Saxton)
7   Time Before, After, Within (David Booth, 1974)
8   Visual Imaging (Based on Heathcote, 1977)

As it is impossible to describe a thought process outside a context, we have chosen to illustrate the models of thinking using 'immigrants' as the source for a class of Grade 8 students (13-year-olds) in their first year of drama.

Dramatic Focus:
> 'Exile is a state of mind which can plague not only those who emigrate but those who remain at home.'
> > Alberto Manguel

The class: 31 students
            Mainstream, semi-urban
            14 first generation Canadians
            15 Canadians
             2 Vietnamese
            12 boys, 19 girls

Social health: generally good, but they are used to 'being taught' and not used to taking responsibility for their own learning.

Students' Personal Luggage: some have heard stories from relatives about immigrating; some have been taken 'home' and have returned; one student has returned to Canada, having been away for three years. They all watch TV. Part of their Social Studies programme is the opening of the Canadian West. Pierre Berton came to the school and talked about the building of the Canadian Pacific Railway. The Vietnamese are children of 'boat people'. Values: middle-class but unquestioning, though the Vietnamese children are unknown factors.

Teacher's Personal Luggage: Honours degree (Physics, Birmingham, England); post-graduate Specialist Certificate in Dramatic Arts, Ontario; granted Canadian citizenship in 1975; maiden name of Italian origin. Enjoys the students, but sometimes impatient with their lack of attack, knows that her migration was easy compared to that of some of her students. Values: middle-class, sometimes a frightening combination of the absolute and the relative. She loves teaching at risk and has a tendency to expect more than she should.

The Play for the Teacher: The combination of Pierre Berton's visit and the approach of Thanksgiving had resulted in an animated

and wide-ranging discussion about travel, turkeys, harvest, The Pilgrim Fathers, the Vikings, the First Peoples and the students' own 'first times'. At the same time, the discussion demonstrated that the students had little real understanding that they were the descendants of immigrants, if not immigrants themselves.
Possible opportunities for learning:

- to have the class work for the first time as a collective
- to provide opportunities for completing tasks important to the drama in small groups
- to find opportunities for reading, writing and, above all, speaking in role
- to find a way to allow the Vietnamese students to make a necessary and positive contribution
- to help the students begin to think dramatically
- to help them sustain their work in role
- to let them see that they are capable of making their own drama.

Taxonomy expectation: The interest is there, the problem is how to rekindle it, and to find the right strategies to encourage their engagement.
Superstructure: 'We are doing a role drama about pioneering on the prairies.'

1   Thematic networking

This initial thinking is brainstorming the idea.

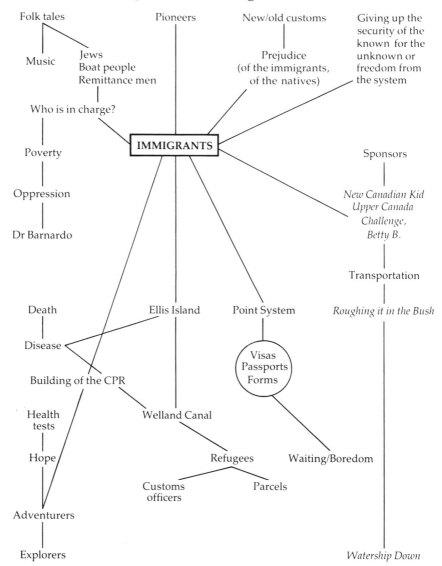

The very act of writing down a brainstorm network lets the teacher see what is in her mind. If the teacher decides to work from a class suggestion, it is useful for the teacher and her students to brainstorm together. The circle represents the teacher's starting point.

Example
Activity: filling in the application forms in the country of origin.
Technique: Teacher in role as secretary at the Consulate.

2 Categorizing

Unlike brainstorming where classification should not be
employed until after the network is laid out, Categorizing starts
with classifications which suggest ideas. After the 'pie' is filled
in, the teacher writes a question for each classification. She then
chooses the question with the most potential and translates it
into the activity.

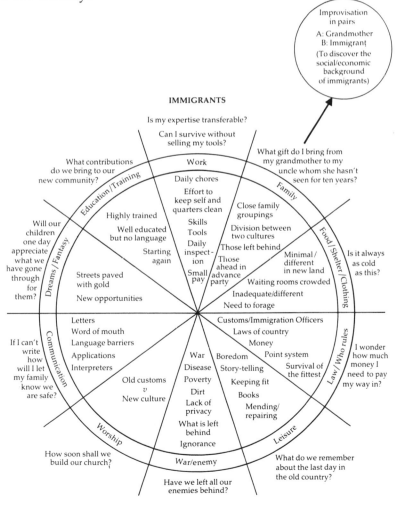

Example
Dramatic Focus: to discover the social/economic background of the immigrants.
Activity: improvising in pairs, A: Grandmother, B: Immigrant

3   The Brotherhoods

The Brotherhoods is a way of looking at the inner experience to find what is common to all human beings in a particular context. This provides the teacher with many analogous situations to draw upon.

- Immigrants are of all those who choose the unknown, for example, explorers, space travellers, pioneers, researchers
- Immigrants are of all those who must carry their possessions with them, for example, nomadic tribes, campers, armed forces, victims of disasters
- Immigrants are of all of those who have to let go and remain behind, for example, mothers, teachers, mourners

The teacher then looks at her students and decides which Brotherhood will act as a starting point for learning. To this class, possessions are very important. The teacher hopes to find out from them what they cannot leave behind and possibly help them to understand that talent, skills and relationships are more important than material possessions (Second Brotherhood).

Example
Technique: Instruction in role: 'Pack a suitcase of these dimensions, 51 cm × 40 cm × 23 cm. You may take only what you can fit inside. I don't know how long the journey will take.'
(Kevin Burns: in a class exploring the Japanese Internment, 1942; Drumheller Drama School, Alberta, 1980.)

4   Man vs man, nature, gods

One of the quickest methods of dramathink is Heathcote's classifications for her declaration that drama is about 'real man in a mess'.[10]

Man vs man: immigrant vs immigrant; immigrant vs inhabitants of the new country; immigrant vs his family who do not want him to leave.

Man vs nature: immigrant vs sea, land, air; immigrant vs the wilderness; immigrant vs an alien environment.

Man vs the gods: immigrant vs immigration officials; immigrant vs the law of the new land; immigrant vs the law of the church.

Illustrations of each of the above are:

- The conflict arising out of the allocation of land.
- The shadow across the sun as the immigrants give thanks for the promised harvest (plague of locusts).
- After a poor harvest, the farmers are still required to give a tithe to the church.

Example
Strategy: Ritual (the giving of the tithes)

5 The reverse

Brian Way in *Development Through Drama* (1967) showed that all drama can be looked at from the opposite side. If students do an exercise in slow motion, ask them to do it in quick motion; if they are doing pair work, A should try it from B's point of view as well as his own. There are two sides to every theme and a good drama teacher should ensure that her students explore both.

- 'Immigrants' is as much about those left behind as it is about those who have left.
- 'Immigrants' is as much about those who are already there as it is about those who are arriving.
- 'Immigrants' is as much about immigrants' prejudice against others as it is about prejudice against them.

Example
The teacher begins by setting up a community in preparation for receiving immigrants. Their first task is to decide in what way(s) immigrants can enhance the community. The immigrants do not appear but send a representative (Stranger in Role) to tell the community why they don't want to become a part of it.

6   The unanswered question

Any topic has questions to which the teacher does not know the answers. Formulating these questions will often suggest appropriate activities and/or foci for exploration.

- What is each immigrant really looking for?
- Could an immigrant ever go back to the old country except in success?
- How did the immigrant survive when he knew so little compared to what we know today?

Example
The third question could become a research project:
What tools did they not have that we have today?
What skills and work habits did they have that we have lost?
Who taught the immigrants how to survive?

7   Time before, after and within

The teacher can use the technique of 'manipulating time' as a method of dramathink.

Time before
(a)   The political situation of the old country
(b)   Choosing which of the family will go to the new country first
(c)   The incident which 'tips the balance' in favour of immigrating

Example
Small group improvising using as a source the letter from the father with money for two members of the family to join him.
Time after
(a)   The day when citizenship is obtained
(b)   The visit of an antique collector (see the second Brotherhood on page 182)
(c)   The new land becomes 'home'

Example
A demonstration of the scene in which the family realizes that the new land is 'home'.

Time within (parallel scenes)
(a)   A discussion among the Customs Officers
(b)   The families left behind
(c)   The work project for which the immigrants are destined

Example
Whole group (Mantle of the Expert) discussion of who will stay
and who will return to the country of origin.

(Early immigrants to Canada were examined for fleas. Those who
had fleas were sent back. 'Imagine', said one student's Russian
grandmother, 'coming all this way to be sent back!')

8   Visual imaging

Visual imaging is akin to the movie in your head or 'seeing with
the mind's eye'. When Heathcote is presented with an idea by
her students she says that she 'flies over it, through it and under
it'. Using this imagery, and with the source in your mind, ask
yourself the following questions:

(a)   What do I see from above? (Example: A long line of people)
(b)   What do I see from below? (Boots)
(c)   What do I see from inside? (Worried faces; the smell of
      humanity)
(d)   What do I see from the outside? (People herded together
      like cattle)

Usually one of the answers will be more strongly 'seen' than the
others, in this case (d). Now ask yourself:

Question	*Answer*
Where am I (above, below, inside, outside)?	Above
What am I doing?	Looking down
What is in my mind?	'Thank God, it's not me down there.'

What am I about to say?	'That's all we're going to process for today. We'll finish them off tomorrow.'
To whom am I speaking?	An underling
How can I take this into drama?	To the whole group: 'We can process no more today. You'll have to make yourselves comfortable for the night. You there, you can hand out the blankets, one per person.'

Although Dorothy appears to start out this way without any prethinking, she is a genius and is probably working in all the thinking models which we have illustrated as well as some that we have not! Those of us who are less gifted need a lot of practice before we are able even to approach that kind of holistic thinking. Whatever dramathink model you use, what you are doing is searching for the collective idea which will generate a collective acceptance – an idea which has potential for action and which intrigues you, and should, on the basis of your knowledge of your students, interest them.

9   The Paradox and the Universal

Within each topic or theme lie the Paradox and the Universal. The teacher should consider them in her initial thinking but not plan for them. As the lesson develops, she should be alert for those Paradoxes and Universals which are revealed. Both are used in the strategy of Reflection, either as a stimulus for discussion, or writing in or out of role, or as a means of synthesizing. For example:

The Paradox: People who emigrate because they cannot wait to get away often turn out to be the strongest proponents of 'the old ways'.
The Universal: We all carry our past into our future.

One of the disadvantages of dramathink is that for some time after a teacher has begun to train herself to think this way, she cannot read or see anything without applying it to drama. 'I just wanted to be entertained,' they complain, 'and I found six really good drama ideas. Let me tell you about them!' Although teachers will never read or see in quite the same way again, practice will make the processes more intuitive, and personal pleasures will accommodate themselves to professional duty!

In conclusion, the only operation that is left for a teacher is the one we briefly touched upon on page 174, Assessment/Evaluation. In our experience it is the one area that teachers find difficult to structure and that administrators require. Perhaps by now you will see that drama, far from being ephemeral, is a process of working which demands skills, intellectual rigour and the infusion of honest feeling. To the teacher who knows what she is doing and why, and who understands what expectations she can have of her students, evaluation and assessment of her students' learning is a natural and necessary accompaniment to the ongoing assessment of her own planning and practice.

Skill-building exercises for teachers

1 Use the models of dramathink to find the 'meat' for role dramas based on the following topics:
(a) Dragons
(b) It's OK to be different
(c) Changing the world
2 Develop the Substructure and the Superstructure for your class.
3 Design the first lesson.
4 Indicate possible extensions for following lessons.

References

1 Part of *On Problems* by Edward Bond
2 Ferguson, M., *The Aquarian Conspiracy*, ch. 9
3 McAra, Don, Drama Department, Christchurch Teacher's College, New Zealand, Thesis (rough copy) p 49, 1983
4 In *Dorothy Heathcote: Drama as a learning medium*, ch 3, pp 34–41, Wagner describes and illustrates splendidly what we have only touched upon here.
5 Koppel, Tiina, 'What is meant by drama in depth?', *FINE Journal*, Alberta, Summer 1982
6 Dodson, Elyse, 'Exploring Social Issues', *Drama and the Whole Curriculum*, pp 97–112
7 Tarlington, C., Verriour, P., 'Role drama from literature', *Offstage*, pp 133–162
8 For a description of this lesson, see *ABCDE Newsletter*, pp 7–10, March/April 1984

9 Schafer, Murray, *When Words Sing*, pp 2, 3
10 *Three Looms Waiting*, BBC Omnibus documentary film, London 1971

_7

Evaluation and assessment

Evaluate: *find numerical expression for*
Assess: *estimate magnitude or quality of*
Oxford Concise Dictionary, 6th Edition (1977)

The matter of evaluation and assessment is a hardy annual in educational debate, and almost every book on drama has a section on it. Despite this attention, many drama educators still find evaluation and assessment difficult to structure. No systematic approach to evaluation in drama has evolved because the subject itself operates in a curriculum model which is heuristic (the pupil is trained to find out things for himself) rather than technological (the student is trained to assimilate a defined body of knowledge). To validate their position, drama teachers are generally required to use closed objective evaluation procedures which restrict them to a partial evaluation of the student. To redress the balance, and in fairness to the student and the teacher, we must adopt a more realistic approach to evaluation.

> 'Education is a process and process inevitably means change . . . It is important that learners and teachers are able to identify change and to know when it has occurred.'[1]

Change is another word for learning, whether it is a five-year-old discovering that one stick plus another stick may be represented by the symbol '2', or a 16-year-old who categorically believes in euthanasia, discovering the weight of professional responsibility and the personal pain in the action of bringing life to an end.[2] In both cases a change has taken place. The five-year-old knows that when he sees the symbol '2' there are two things involved. If he can write down '2' when the teacher asks how many eyes he has, he is correct and is demonstrating his learning. The 16-year-old student has been given a role drama experience in which the teacher's Dramatic Focus was to explore the implications of euthanasia for the professionals involved. The student's role writing revealed some change in understanding and the reflective out of role discussion allowed him to recognize that he had changed. Until he faces a situation (as did the five-year-old) where he can apply this learning (for example, an aged grandparent ill with terminal cancer) neither he nor the teacher can verify that this change in understanding has 'taken'.

In other words, we can evaluate the five-year-old because he is either right or wrong. We can give him a numerical expression for his learning, 10 out of 10 or 0 out of 10, meaning he knows it or he does not know it. But what do we do about giving a mark for the work of the 16-year-old? We can only estimate the depths of his new understanding through his writing and speaking in conjunction with his contributions within the role drama.

In drama, it is important to know what things can, according to the definition, be evaluated and what things can be assessed. Criteria for objective evaluation can be stated in behavioural terms, for example, the student will write in role, whereas criteria for assessment are more open to interpretation, for example, the student will express his concerns through role writing. Assessment, therefore, takes into account the subjective nature of the assessor (the teacher) and for that reason it needs to be balanced by the contribution of the one who is being assessed (the student). With young students, the teacher can give them the opportunity to talk about their work and their contributions within the role drama (see Chapter 4, page 79). With more mature students, their assessments can be given in written form or in discussion with the teacher. Whatever procedure is chosen, the student must be aware of the criteria that have been established.

Criteria for evaluation and assessment

It should be noted that the objectives in the following sections have been selected from a wide range of books, articles, guidelines and discussions with teachers, and are by no means comprehensive.

Evaluation

Evaluation is employed in looking at work in the expressive frame. It is summative, that is, it occurs at the end of a unit of work. The criteria for evaluating are instructional, behavioural and prescriptive. They suggest a homogeneity of outlook and operate by applying a set of common standards to a product. Thus:

- Evaluation occurs at, and is completed within, a specific time.
- The marking scheme is predetermined.
- There must have been an instructional learning time prior to the evaluation.
- In evaluation the outcome must be predictable: the teacher will know what outcomes she is expecting and she should share these with her students. A predicted outcome may be a part of or the only criterion for valuing.

Areas of evaluation in which 'specific judgements' may be made are administrative, content and skills. Some examples of objectives are given below:

Administrative
Criteria are established at the beginning of the year and generally remain constant. They may be based upon:

1 *Attendance*
- The student is not only present but ready to begin work.
- If the student is unavoidably absent, he is able to re-enter the class with a minimum of disruption.
- The student is present throughout the class.

2 *Punctuality*
- The student is not only on time, but ready to begin.
- If the student is unavoidably late, he is able to fit in with a minimum of disruption.

3 *Respect for space*
- The student keeps things in their proper place.
- The student takes responsibility for restoring the room to the accepted working design at the beginning and end of the lesson.

- The student treats the room as a 'professional space' (learning environment).

4 *Respect for Equipment*
- The student uses the equipment as instructed.
- The student replaces equipment neatly.

5 *Completing class assignments*
- The work is on time.
- The work is neat (the teacher must establish what *she* means by neat!).
- The work must be grammatically and stylistically correct.

6 *Following instructions*
- The student does what he is told.
- The student works quickly and quietly (if appropriate).

Content
Content refers to the development of a body of objective knowledge.

1 *Knowing the rules of the game*
- The student demonstrates good class discipline (the teacher must establish her criteria for this).
- The student knows what is involved in role drama.
- The student knows what is meant by terms such as: 'mime', 'improvise'.

2 *Knowing the vocabulary of the theatre*
- The student knows what is meant by artistic vocabulary: 'tension', 'symbol', 'aesthetic'.
- The student knows what is meant by technical vocabulary: 'fresnel', 'apron', 'tape loop'.
- The student knows what is meant by administrative vocabulary: 'front of house', 'producer', 'promotion'.

3 *Knowing the history of the theatre*
- The student knows the characteristics of Greek theatre, epic theatre, naturalistic theatre.

4 *Knowing the literature of the theatre*
- The student reads criticism, biography, plays.
- The student attends theatre events.

Skills
Skills are the demonstration of 'knowledge about' through action.

● The student 'mimes' without talking.
● The student knows when to speak, when to remain silent and when to listen.
● The student speaks from memory.
● The student improvises.
● The student uses the vocabulary of the theatre correctly.
● The student employs the media in the service of the drama (mask, costume, prop).
● The student maintains a role.

All of the above can be given a numerical value, but the teacher must consider carefully what it is she is marking. For example, can she give 10 out of 10 to a student who maintains his role, without being influenced by the quality of his contributions? If not, then this criterion belongs under assessment.

If the teacher evaluates objectively, then she must clarify the allocation of marks before the exercise or event, so that the student can share in the responsibility of controlling the outcome.

What are the implications of this kind of evaluation?
1   There is a danger that the student will only be exposed to that kind of drama work which the teacher knows well and for which she feels she can construct criteria.
2   It implies a pre-arranged and narrowly defined curriculum of work, which is teacher imposed. This is in contradiction to the philosophy that drama is a student-centred learning activity.
3   It implies a sense of resolution, of 'finish' that, having learned this, there is nowhere else to go. We frequently hear students say, 'We've *done* mime. We've *done* mirrors'. They are unable to conceive of these theatrical forms as practical tools to use, for instance, in interpretation of a written source.
4   It encourages drama teachers to ignore, at their peril, Robinson's (1980) reminder that 'Absolute objectives is as much a phantom as value-free evaluation.'
5   Summative evaluation looks only at the surface or 'demonstration' aspects of the art form and fails to consider the interpretive, affective or social experiences inherent in drama work.
6   Summative evaluation negates the collective power of the group. In so doing, it precludes the teacher's intuitive inclination to assess the influence and consequent effectiveness arising from

the group dynamic which, in this case, is the action of the student on the group and the group on the student. It is like evaluating the individual soccer player without taking into account the assistance he receives from the rest of the team in order to put the ball in the net.[3]

However, we must face reality. At report card time 'the teacher must systematically boil down the student's creativity into a numerical broth and measure it up against a percentage rank chart.'[4] But if objective evaluation criteria are used exclusively, we are ignoring the holistic nature of drama. We must be careful, as Koestler warns, of the myth that the only scientific method worth that name is quantitative measurement. To believe that, he says, is to run the risk of losing Man in the process.[5] Fortunately, enlightened educators now recognize that there is a qualitative dimension to learning which must be considered if the student's work is to be fairly judged. Drama teachers will recognize the characteristics of qualitative methods:

- the focus is on a different 'way' of knowing, based on involvement in the experience.
- the particular event or situation must be viewed as a part of a whole and not in isolation.
- the logic is inductive, that is, the study of the particular builds towards the universal.
- the events can only be described after the participants have experienced them.
- qualitative work is the study of things *as they are*.[6]

Releasing the pressure on the teacher to evaluate only by quantitative measurement means that she is free to formulate criteria which will help her to estimate the quality of the learning.

Assessment

While assessment may be used to look at the quality of work in the expressive frame, it is the *only* way of looking at students' work appropriate for the meaning frame. The criteria for assessment are descriptive, invitational[6] and evocative. They encompass a diversity of experiences and are designed to reveal both significance in, and the uniqueness of, a variety of products. Features of assessment are:

- Assessment is an ongoing process.
- In assessment, although the teacher may *expect* an outcome, she cannot, because of the nature of the work, *predict* an outcome.
- An 'appropriate response' presupposes that the responder has a number of experiences to choose from.
- The criteria in assessment identify the task, situation, problem and the potential learning outcomes that may be expected.

Some areas which may be assessed by the qualitative method are: the general development of the individual and the group; working in role; reflection.

Some examples of assessment criteria
General
These may apply either in or out or role.
The student:

- works seriously with purpose and self-discipline.
- is willing to trust the teacher and peers.
- integrates skills learned from other subject areas and previous drama work into new work.
- channels and fuses creative energy to explore form and meaning collectively.[7]
- initiates and extends ideas.
- selects actions and words that enhance the significance of the experience for himself and others and can apply this skill to work in script or source.
- is sensitive to the needs and contributions of others within the group (he is listening, responding, suggesting, rather than talking and 'laying down the law').
- makes decisions and thinks through the implications and consequences.
- has the courage to risk in order to experience.
- has the courage to fail.
- is prepared to take responsibility for the work (even when it goes wrong).
- accepts deferment (he works to gain future satisfaction).
- perceives work as a process not a product. (He works with critical awareness, sums up, assesses, deduces, analyzes, and uses the new information as part of the new situation.)

- is aware of form. (He selects and retains focus, injects and sustains tension.)
- communicates meaning to an audience when working in a performance mode.
- does not work only for himself but supports the work of his peers.

Working in role
The student:

- expresses himself in the appropriate category of identification.
- is working towards a rich level of personal engagement. (He finds a feeling quality appropriate to the context.[8])
- maintains class discipline within the role.
- uses appropriate language (verbal and non-verbal) and behaviour (giving and receiving of signals) when working in role.
- infuses the role with appropriate energy.
- expresses believable points of view and attitudes in appropriate language through role play.

Reflection
This area makes an important contribution to the total picture of a student's attainment.
The student:

- reflects on the meanings created in the drama during and after the experience.
- reconsiders values and attitudes.
- articulates shifts or changes in understanding and can reflect on the work through another medium (discussion, writing, art or another dramatic genre).
- assesses the work and his own contribution to it (self-evaluation).
- uses his learning to evaluate the teacher's contribution.

All of the above can be rated subjectively and reasonably accurately by a letter grade.

A   for very good work
B   for good work
C   for adequate work
D   for unsatisfactory work

E for unacceptable work (Withdrawal recommended but only after the teacher has analyzed her relationship with the student at both the personal and the work level.)

A teacher must decide for herself (or it may be decided for her by the school's administration) what she means by each letter grade and she should clarify her criteria with her students at the beginning of the year. Assessment is formative, and as such should incorporate the active participation of the student as well as the teacher.

Formative assessment occurs in a number of ways:

1 At 'check points' within the drama work or role drama. These are times when the teacher stops the drama:

- for clarification ('Out of role for a minute. Do we all know what's going on here?')
- for direction ('What scene do you think we need to look at now?')
- for evaluation ('Are you satisfied that this is how a ruler should look/behave/speak?')

2 In out of role discussion. This occurs within the drama class when the students and teacher reflect upon the work attempted.

3 In out of class discussion on a one-to-one basis. This is the student–teacher interview when the student is invited by the teacher to contribute his view of his progress. (See Appendix 2 for examples of self-assessment forms.)

These opportunities allow both student and teacher to clarify what has been learned and identify those areas of learning which still need attention.

The implications of formative assessment

Too often the teacher thinks solely in terms of assessing her students. But she cannot do this fairly unless she first assesses her lesson plan (Were the strategies, techniques and activities appropriate?) and the implementation of that plan (Was she flexible enough to adapt her plan to include the ideas from the students?) to see whether the objectives she had for her students were appropriately supported by her teaching.

Because of the collective nature of drama, the individual is often 'lost' in the group. It is unrealistic to expect a drama teacher to 'see' every student in every class every day. Assessment is formative, that is, cumulative and on-going, so the teacher must make time to maintain an assessment journal in which she notes student progress, her diagnosis of student problems, and an assessment of her own work. One teacher we know selects two students to assess at one time in each class and manages to do this for every student in the class three times a term.

The teacher can be accused of unfairness. She and her students must grow to trust her subjective judgement, based on careful planning and a clear statement of the standards to be maintained.

By concentrating on the affective domain, the teacher can neglect the importance of the work in the expressive frame.

In the interests of not interfering with 'creativity', the teacher is often afraid to demand standards.

However, in spite of all of these negative implications of the process of assessment (and to recognize them is to be part way towards solving them), assessment is a vital component of a lesson. It helps the teacher know where to go next and gives evidence of student development throughout the unit, month or term depending upon how frequently assessment is made.

Contemplative assessment

At the beginning of this chapter (page 190) we said that learning often cannot be verified until it can be seen to inform the student's thinking in a different situation (the 16-year-old and his grandparent). We call this kind of verification contemplative assessment.[9] This type of assessment cannot be given a letter grade or a numerical mark, but the teacher must not ignore its importance because it demonstrates the application of the student's learning to his life, which is the major goal of education.

The nature of contemplative assessment is that:

- it occurs outside the drama and thus outside the time-frame of drama. The important factor to consider here is that it cannot in any way change the nature of the dramatic experience itself but is a result of it.
- both the teacher and the student must have shared a mutual, personal involvement in the experience.
- the information is volunteered by the student and demonstrates that the experience has 'settled' or 'sifted down'.
- it may be revealed during an interview, through a casual remark, through the student's comment about a source (book,

poem, newspaper article) which relates to the experience and which provided the opportunity for the learning.

- it may be revealed in casual remarks from a teaching colleague which indicate a connection made by the student between the drama experience and another subject area.
- it may be revealed when the student uses his learning in a previous drama/theatre experience to make a new statement in drama/theatre form.
- it may be revealed by the student's behaviour in the play-ground, in the cafeteria or at school events.
- it may be revealed in conversation with parents.

Although contemplative assessment appears to be of no direct use to the students and no particular help to the teacher's marking, its has a tendency to show itself at the most appropriate moments. Just when you are beginning to wonder if you would not be more suited to sheep farming, a colleague tells you that your most difficult class has shed a new light on his history programme as a result of their role drama exploring 'Gandhi'. You read in a newspaper's entertainment section that a student you fought for 15 years ago is now Hollywood's golden boy. An old student meets you on the street, reminds you of a lesson which you cannot recall at all and tells you that it changed his life. The rewards of teaching and learning can be a long time coming but when they do, they confirm what you sometimes doubt. Something did happen! Someone did learn! Maybe you can teach, after all!

Examples of the evaluation/assessment process

We will now examine in some detail the evaluation/assessment process as it applies to Drama as Method, Drama as Subject and Drama as Product.

Example 1   Drama as Method

In Chapter 6 on planning, there is an example of the teacher's plan, implementation and assessment ('Big Rigs', pages 173–176). Let us suppose that the teacher decides to evaluate and assess George and Mary in Day 1 of 'Big Rigs'. (See table on next page.)

Drama as Method
Role drama: 'Big Rigs' Day 1

What is to be evaluated	George	Comments	Mary	Comments
Attendance: (10)	10		10	
Punctuality: (10)	10		10	
Working within focus (designing): (10)	10		5	Slow to start
Copying from the board: (10)	7	Left words out	8	Did not finish
Total marks out of 40:	37		33	
What is to be assessed				
Level of Personal Engagement:	B	Committed	C	Barely engaged
Appropriate behaviour:				
● class discipline within the role	A		A	
● maintaining a role	B		C	She tried but had difficulty
● behaving as professional	A		C	
Appropriate language:	A		C	Tried (after being corrected by example)
Participation in discussion:				
● contributing	B+	Sound!	C	Answered only when directly spoken to
● listening to others	B−	Prefers to talk!	B−	Appeared to listen!
Application to task:	A		C	Slow starter, always wants me to check her work
Giving and taking directions:	B	Over-anxious to start	C	Can take directions – will she ever be able to give any?
Working independently:	A		B	OK when she gets going
Working cooperatively:	B	Does not suffer fools gladly	–	Cannot assess
Making decisions:	B	Does not consider implications	–	Cannot assess

Teacher's thinking about her evaluation/assessment of George and Mary

Evaluation

It is easy for Mary to get full marks for attendance and punctuality; she is never absent and always on time. George has terrible home problems and is often away or late.

Mary is mentally lethargic, so copying is not a hazard for her.

So far George has only 4 more marks than Mary although his work is of a totally different order from Mary's, which is not revealed by the evaluation.

Assessment

George is somewhere between an A and a B, Mary between a C and a D, which is appropriate for their work in class. But consider what happened at break (page 173).

Contemplative assessment

Can I take what Mary said into consideration? What if George made a comment and I didn't hear it?

Teacher's summary in her assessment journal (mark book)

George   November 12, Big Rigs, B+
Really working well on all cylinders and his engagement in the drama contained his aggressive behaviour.

Mary   November 12, Big Rigs, C− → C
Did everything but *so* slowly. On the other hand she obviously was strongly engaged (break). Good work!

Assessment, as we have said, requires student input, but because George and Mary are 'slow learners' they are rarely able to assess their work objectively. However, out of role, George contributed to the discussion, initiated by Andrew, on what made the drama 'good' and the teacher could have given them the opportunity to talk about their work and their contributions within the role drama. For example: the teacher in role as a prospective buyer draws evaluation from the students: 'Now, Mr Sparrow (George), what do you consider to be the special feature of your design? How would it benefit the driver?'

Drama is about a shift or change in understanding. What shift or change was there in Day 1 of Big Rigs? The teacher was not really expecting any at such an early stage in the drama, but one occurred: 'They were worried at the end of the day about the safety of their designs.' (page 173). For the first time all year, the class showed a respect for their work and the beginnings of an understanding of the problems of 'the one who invents'. This change from indifference to concern about their work can be assessed collectively and becomes part of the teacher's learning about the social health of the class.

'Big Rigs' is an example of Drama as Method, therefore the assessment/evaluation of the drama work must be linked to the learning objectives of the Educational Context (Language Arts), and the Educational Focus (creative writing). The teacher received eight different kinds of writing from the students in fifteen lessons over a period of four weeks:

1 Copying lists of ideas from the blackboard for later reference (individual).
2 Writing 'lock-up procedures' on newsprint (whole class).
3 Deciding on the format of a security pass (whole class). Designing the security pass (individual).
4 Writing, in role, a diary entry describing the events of the security check. (A very tense day as the 'design studio' appeared to have been broken into) (individual).
5 Writing, in role, a critique of the performance of the safety features which they themselves had designed (individual).
6 Writing a promotional description of their Big Rig to be bound into a catalogue (individual).
7 Writing a letter requesting space for their Big Rig display at the Automotive Shows across the country (groups of three).
8 Responding by letter to a request from the Heavy Duty Truck Division of General Motors for the rights to build 'Big Rig Safetys' (whole class creating, individual appointed to write the courteous refusal! See Appendix 3).

It is interesting to note that the quality of the writing was in direct relation to the quality of the drama and the level of engagement of the students. For example, number 5 above. After a weekend break the teacher re-engaged the students through voice-over as the students took their rigs on to the road for testing. Questioning in role after the physical activity (broken by demonstrations from some of the students) resulted in an experience which was strong enough to enable the students to write at this sophisticated level. Also, in number 4 above, the kind of writing the teacher was looking for required her to plan and execute a lesson which would be full of tension.

The teacher's choice of strategies and techniques generated

great interest in the students which resulted in some remarkable pieces of writing.

Summary
Evaluation/assessment is controlled by:
- the success of the plan and its implementation (the quality of the drama) which directly influences
- the performance of the student which, in turn, influences
- the degree to which the educational objectives are accomplished.

When drama is used as method, the content is guided by the subject being taught. When drama *is* the subject to be taught, the content is guided by the demands of the drama curriculum.

Example 2 Drama as Subject

Substructure: see Chapter 6, page 168, example 1 for information.
Number in class: 25 (10 boys, 15 girls)
Place: drama studio
Time: 1.30 to 3.00 pm
Educational Context: Drama
Educational Focus: Improvisation
Dramatic Context: Building a biography through a sitting-down drama
Superstructure: 'We wrote a play together.'

Assessment in teacher's journal (Lesson 1)
The gift-giving exercises showed the teacher that although the class could think carefully about their gifts and they demonstrated good skills in the exchange part of the exercise, they could not see the significance and the potential of their ideas. Some examples of the work:

1 Paul gave Angela a pram as a wedding present. (Angela had come back from the holiday engaged to be married.) Angela returned the pram saying, 'There's no point in me keeping it. Peter has made it quite clear that he doesn't want children.'
2 David gave John weight-lifting equipment. (John had put on seven pounds over Christmas.) John returned it saying, 'The landlord won't allow heavy equipment in the apartment.'

3   Alison gave Martyn an hour-glass. (Martyn's New Year resol-
    ution is to be on time for every class this term.) Martyn
    returned it saying, 'I've just been told I have only six months
    to live. I don't want to have anything that will remind me of
    time passing.'
    (The class laughed at the 'clever' reason for the refusal but
    missed the significance of the meaning.)

Planning for the next lesson:

New Play for the Teacher
In addition to honest work from the whole group working
together, the teacher wants her students to see how rich their
ideas are for exploration (an important aspect of improvisation).
Source
The teacher selects number 3 because it has 'weight' and because
time is a problem for most of us.
Activity
She chooses Sitting-Down Drama because it requires the students
to take the initiative in the story-building and takes the focus
away from 'doing' (expressive frame).
Note
She reminds herself to ask the students to suggest names other
than Alison and Martyn for the protagonists in order to release
the story from those students to the group.

Activity
Sitting-down drama

Dramatic Focus
To explore the source and discover the story behind it.

Strategy
Improvisation

Techniques
Teacher as facilitator. Introduce source, set up investigation.

Administration
Chairs in a close circle.

Questions
1   What names shall we give the two people?
2   What scene shall we look at first?
3   Who will volunteer to take on the roles for us?

Because the drama is in *their* hands, it is unwise and pointless

to plan further. However, the teacher must understand her functions in a sitting-down drama as questioner, synthesizer, commentator and builder of the awareness of dramatic potential.
Conclusion
By 2.30: 'We have only time for one more scene. Which one *must* we see?'
Reflection
Probably writing in role, the kind to be determined by the last scene. Discussion?

For a description of this lesson see Chapter 2, pages 26–27. For a student's description see Appendix 4.

Assessment in teacher's journal (Lesson 2)
Interest
Intrigued both by the nature of the activity and their own abilities to make a story out of nothing. Fair amount of 'ham' from Lance and his group to begin with. Tony left half way through (his uncle is dying) but Tony is OK – sensible boy.
Improvisation skills
They are surprised at the depth of their feelings and very proud. They handled Lance and the group well, loved working together and respected each other's contributions. Saw the difference between the rather superficial beginning (always like this!) and the amazing honesty of the last few scenes. Quality of the in-role writing responds exactly to the quality of the drama (and all thanks to them, not me!).
Note
I had them all into Jane's head after the scene where she was sent home from work and got them to turn their chairs away from the circle. When we got to the last scene they suggested we do the same so that the two in the scene were not inhibited by us. I think they've got it! Clever things! Must remember to tell them what it was that was good – unless, of course, they tell me first!
Tom and Bella want to script it – think about that? Do I want to spoil a good thing by using it to mess around with?

Teacher's thinking about her evaluation/assessment of Lance and Martyn (See next page.)
Evaluation
Martyn always comes prepared to work and works consistently. Lance has to be seduced into work. The latter part of the lesson he really came through – thanks to the rest of the class. Martyn

Drama as Subject
Improvisation: Sitting-down drama   Day 2

What is to be evaluated	Lance	Comments	Martyn	Comments
Attendance: (10)	9	Grudging	10	
Punctuality: (10)	10		7	Late again!
Respect for space and equipment: (5)	2½	Belongings spread around	5	
Rules of the game/following instructions: (5)	4	Chatting	5	
Homework: (5)	2	Messy journal	5	Impeccable
Total marks out of 35:	27½		31	

What is to be assessed	Lance	Comments	Martyn	Comments
Level of Personal Engagement:	C → B+	Barely engaged to Committing	B+	Committed?
Expression of feeling:	A	A way with words	B+	Real concern
Work as process:	B	Product-oriented	B+	
Maintaining role:	C → A−	From the superficial to the real, even when we are not watching!	B	Likes to feel safe
Energy applied appropriately:	C	When it suits him	A+	
Expressing in another medium:	C	Thin! Does not see this as a way of being 'seen'.	B+	Thoughtful but dull

has 3½ more than Lance, which hardly seems fair considering how much help he gave him. Thank heaven, I don't have to depend solely upon evaluation!

Assessment
Lance lies between a C and a B, Martyn lies between a B+ and an A, which, translated into numbers for school administration, is:
Lance = 65/100 or 32½/50
Martyn = 80/100 or 40/50
Evaluation plus assessment (35 + 50 = 85):
Lance: 27½ plus 32½ = 60/85
Martyn: 31 plus 40 = 71/85
(What is missing here is the 15% allotted to the student's self-evaluation.)

Teacher's summary in her assessment journal (mark book)

Lance   January 22, Improvisation (Sitting-down drama)
            60/85, Lance's marks for himself: —/15, Total ——.
            Lance works well when he is 'on show' and when he feels like it. This particular work involved 'showing'.
Martyn   January 22, Improvisation (Sitting-down drama)
            71/85, Martyn's marks for himself: —/15, Total——.
            Martyn works well. Still some concern about the intensity of his involvement. Be sure to check for this in his role writing and journal.

Because the teacher had chosen to evaluate/assess these two students, she made a point of seeing them individually in the next week to have their assessment of their work, based on the criteria they had received at the beginning of the term.

Was there any shift or change in understanding in this lesson that the teacher could identify? The students realized that they were capable of working over an extended period of time at something which they themselves were creating. They recognized that their involvement in the work was of a different kind from anything they had done before and it became a 'yardstick' for future work (contemplative assessment).

As in Drama as Method, the assessment/evaluation of drama work must be linked to the learning objectives of the Educational Focus: Improvisation.

Specific areas of assessment for Improvisation
Pre-Improvisation
- Quality of discussion about the source
- Negotiation of meaning about the source
- What is used to recreate the setting
- Casting of the roles
- Finding the beginning
- Use of time
- Willingness to take risks
- Respect for each other

Improvising
- Appropriate representation of role through language and movement
- Use of theatrical elements and form (shaping the work)
- Spontaneity of response to the situation
- Manipulating the 'givens' (who? where? when? what?) in order to discover the why?
- Recognizing a non-productive situation and remedying it within the improvisation
- Respect for the material
- Respect for each other in role
- Recognizing when the improvisation is complete

Post-Improvisation
- Quality of the reflection (spoken and/or written)
- Willingness to share reflection in whole group
- Willingness to accept others' experiences as equally valid
- Willingness to re-improvise from a new or different perspective

Summary
The work of the collective demonstrated that they were capable of meeting the objectives with the teacher as facilitator. The next step would be to see how they apply the skills they used as a group when working in smaller groups without the teacher's direct involvement. At that point she would be better able to assess individual development.

The teacher, having looked at the Social Health of the class and their Personal Luggage, judged that they were ready to move beyond role drama into an activity which required them to assume the responsibility which she had previously held in role.

Her timing, together with her choice of source and her questioning skills, promoted improvisational work of a high standard.

Example 3   Drama as Product

Grade 11 (16-year-olds)
Number in class: 22 (9 boys and 13 girls in 3 groups)
Educational Context: Drama
Educational Focus: Theatre for children
Dramatic Context: Devising a 'play' for elementary school children
Dramatic Focus: To explore and employ previous learning in a performance mode
Substructure:
Social Health: They work well with each other, although there is still a tendency to 'clique'.

Teacher's Personal Luggage: Experience as a drama teacher with younger children. She has worked with a children's theatre company, and has observed, as a part of the audience, many children's theatre programmes.

Content: This will come from group discussion, discussion with the teacher and interaction with the children for whom they will be performing.

Students' Personal Luggage: They are experienced in performance and possess a fair degree of theatre skills and writing skills.

Play for the Teacher: To fulfil the curriculum requirements:

- to demonstrate the demands a young audience will make upon the performers.
- to have the students read and study a wide range of material.
- to employ the appropriate theatrical devices and techniques in rehearsal.
- to select the appropriate theatrical forms for the material.

Taxonomy expectation: Evaluation

Superstructure: 'We are making and touring a play for kids.'

In evaluation/assessment as it applies to a product, there are three problems for the teacher:

1   The major criterion will be the successful presentation of the group's work to an audience.
2   She will be assessing/evaluating the group as well as the individual.
3   She must decide for herself how much of the product is dependent upon the process.

When the major criterion is that of a product before an audience, it is part of the responsibility of the teacher to make sure that the students do not go before an audience, especially of children, until they have the appropriate skills. At the same time it must be remembered that a great deal of useful learning can occur through failure. It is the teacher's responsibility to know if the students are mature enough to learn from their experience.

In evaluating product we suggest you turn to pages 191 to 193 for a selection of criteria suggestions. Pages 195 to 196 are useful in suggesting criteria for assessment.

Other points that should be considered

The group dynamic
- How well does the group work independently of the teacher?
- What about the group which settles for the 'easy way out'?
- What about the group with the marvellous ideas but not enough time to realize them?
- What about the group that messes around, but somehow manages to produce a reasonable piece of work?
- What about the group that has nobly carried a 'dead weight'?

The teacher's input
- How much of the group's success is dependent upon the teacher's contribution?
- How much of the group's failure is a result of the teacher's failure to intervene at the appropriate moment?
- How ready is the group to accept the responsibility of failure and to learn from it?

The quality of the product
- How suitable was the choice of material?
- How appropriate were the theatrical frames for the abilities of the group?

- How effective was the meaning communicated through the form?
- How flexible was the product in adapting to the variety of playing spaces and audiences?
- How well did the promotional material demonstrate the relationship between expectation and satisfaction?

Student evaluation and assessment
The students' evaluation and assessment of their work may take a number of forms:

1 The Daily Journal: a documentation of what has happened and a reflection upon the process and the performances.
2 The Script: this will include, besides the script, technical cue sheets and stage management concerns, as well as promotional materials, schedules, etc.
3 Self-assessment/evaluation forms: the student's own evaluation of his personal contributions towards maintaining the task and the social health of the group.
4 Group evaluation/assessment forms: each student's responses to the work of the other members of the group and the success of the group's interactive processes. (See Appendix 2a.)

A suggested format for individual, subjective assessment
In groups we all play a number of roles. The list below identifies some of these roles. Which roles did you play and when? Which roles were new to you and how comfortable did you feel using them?

Leader by choice: You know what leadership involves and you are prepared to take on that responsibility.
Leader by election: You are good at leading and your group recognized this *or* you are difficult if you are not allowed to lead and your group recognized this.
Leader by default: You sensed that someone had to take over before it was too late and you were prepared to take on that responsibility.
Positive follower: You are supportive and encouraging to all ideas, even ones you think may not work.
Ideas person: You are prepared to give your ideas. You often have a practical follow-through to support your concepts. You are not offended if your ideas are not picked up.

Negative follower: You are more comfortable simply to go along, and you do not find many occasions when you want to offer ideas.

Iconoclast: You have lots of ideas, some of them unusual, but you are unable to offer constructive suggestions for their implementation.

Absentee: You cannot be counted upon, but you do expect to be included in the final product.

Nurturer: You see that the social health of the group is an important part of accomplishing the tasks and make sure that it is maintained.

Doer: You are prepared to do what is asked of you, even if it means working outside class time and in your own time after school. (See Appendix 2b for a chart example.)

Some suggestions for marking group projects

1 The project is worth 7 out of 10. Everyone in the group receives 70%.
2 The project is worth 70%. A group of 6, for example, has an aggregate of 420 marks (6 × 70). These marks (420) are to be shared amongst the group, so that at least one member gets 80% or over and at least one gets 60% or under. Mark allocation is accompanied by comments when handed in to the teacher.
3 The group marks each individual in the group through discussion. Each mark is supported by intelligent comments and submitted in writing to the teacher.

Conclusion

Evaluation and assessment are not 'chores' to be undertaken at the mad whim of an insensitive school administrator. They are integral components of the teacher's planning, without which she cannot know where to go next. They tell the student where he stands so that he can share responsibility for his own learning. Above all, evaluation and assessment reveal to the teacher both the value and the quality of her teaching.

Skill-building exercises for the teacher

'Because the process of education is the assumption that it is a purposeful activity which manifests itself through the intervention of teachers in the lives and development of learners, the teacher in the evaluative process must look at herself.'[10]

1 Have I communicated my expectations to the class?
2 Are my expectations vested in the meaningful world of the student?
3 Am I still working on first impressions?
4 Has the nature of my students' dependence changed from that of passive dependence where I am seen to be 'in authority' to an active dynamic dependence where I am seen to be 'an authority'?[10]
5 How are the students different after their experiences with me in drama?
6 What thinking, feeling and skills have I facilitated?
7 Are my students able to identify those thoughts, feelings and skills?
8 Have I demanded enough of my students?
9 Have I demanded enough of myself?
10 Am I pulling out old material without adapting it to the needs of my present students?
11 Have I shown a willingness to change, adapt, stop when I could not see any learning taking place?
12 What strategies and techniques have I used in my teaching in the last month? Am I over-using any? Is it because I feel safe with them?
13 Do I vary ways of Reflection?
14 Do I ask productive questions?
15 What roles have I taken? Am I still clinging to Authority?
16 Have I given the students satisfying experiences? Do they come eagerly to class?
17 Have I shared with my colleagues what I am doing in order to provide opportunities for interdisciplinary work, to clear up misconceptions and maintain the 'profile' of drama?
18 Am I making full use of the resources in the community, human and informational?
19 Am I keeping up with the latest writing and attending conferences?
20 Am I offering to share my expertise?
21 Have I discussed something other than drama with a teacher other than a drama teacher?
22 Have I read a book, been to a concert, seen a play or a film? Have I made something? Have I done something for myself?

The demands on a drama teacher, or any teacher for that matter, are great. A good teacher's understanding of her teaching responsibilities must include a recognition of the important part her personal life plays in her professional performance.

References

 1   Davies, Haydn, 'An operational approach to evaluation,' in *Issues in Educational Drama*, Day, C. and Norman, J., eds, The Falmer Press, London 1983
 2   Morgan, N. H., Saxton, J. M., 'Structures, strategies and techniques', *CCYDA Journal*, Winter 1983
 3   Burke, M. and Saxton, J., 'Evaluation in drama? Yes!', *ABCDE Journal*, vol. 6, no. 1, 1984
 4   Matlock, Tim, 'Let's evaluate assessment!', *ABCDE Journal*, vol. 6, no. 1, June, 1984
 5   Koestler, Arthur, Transcript of the Alpbach Symposium: 'Beyond reductionism: new perspectives in the life sciences'. (Four Pillars of Unwisdom)
 6   Rist, Ray, 'On the application of ethnographic inquiry to education: procedures and possibilities', *Journal of Research in Science Teaching*, vol. 19, no. 6, pp 439–450, 1982
 7   Cook, Pat, 'Evaluating drama', *2D*, vol. 2, no. 1, Summer 1982
 8   Davies, Haydn, 'Learning goals and personal antonomy', *Drama Broadsheet*, vol. 1, no. 1, Autumn 1983
 9   Burke, M. and Saxton, J., 'Evaluation in drama? Yes!', *ABCDE Journal*, vol. 6, no. 1, 1984
10   Davies, Haydn, 'An operational approach to evaluation', in *Issues in Educational Drama*, Day, C. and Norman, J., eds, The Falmer Press, London 1983

Epilogue

Scene: A room in what could be a community centre. A group of 22 people are sitting on hard chairs facing a leader. Although the atmosphere would suggest that these people have met before, one can see from their positions that there is considerable anxiety and some distress. The leader has a pile of folders beside her, but she does not refer to them.

Leader: 'Did any of you know or suspect anything about your child before you were told?'

Parent 1: 'I was shocked because our daughter had tried this before and we thought we'd worked it out (she turns to man beside her), didn't we?'

Parent 2: 'I had no idea my child would do that. We're an ordinary family and I never expected it.'

Parent 3: (Belligerently) 'I was really upset that he'd be so stupid. He must have been conned into it.'

Parent 4: 'I wasn't really surprised. I'm divorced and I work a lot. We don't have much time together and I know he's been confused.'

Leader: 'Mrs Howard mentioned why she thought her son had turned to drugs. What do the rest of you think might be the reason your children became involved.'

Parent 3: (Still belligerent) 'I feel my son has just been hanging around with the wrong people.'

Parent 5: 'I think our daughter did it to be popular. She never had many friends before.'

Parent 4: 'I think my son was angry at me. My husband and I just broke up and he blames me. Maybe he wanted to get back at me.'

Leader: 'What are your main concerns now?'

Parent 3: 'I am really mad! I'd like to give him a good beating.'

Parent 6: 'No, I'm not mad, but I am sad that she'd be so stupid.

We'll really have to have a good talk about it, won't we Amy?'

Parent 4: 'I feel guilty. I knew he was upset about Jim and me and I just let him go his own way and didn't talk to him enough.'

Parent 7: 'I'm angry at myself because I didn't find out sooner. I don't know why she didn't talk to us about her problem.'

This excerpt could be from a script in which a social worker is counselling a group of parents whose children are involved in drugs. In fact, this is a record of a class of 8–10 year old children who had chosen to explore 'Teenagers and Drugs' for their drama experience. The students were in role as the parents and the teacher was in role as a social worker.

Later, when everyone was out of role, the teacher commented casually, 'Wow, it's hard work being a parent!' Some responses were:

'I was really concerned.'

'I didn't know it would be so hard to control your child.'

'I liked feeling grown-up at the meeting.'

'I'd never thought about it before but the words spilled out as if they'd always been there.'

'I was calm as a parent and that's the way I'd want to be.'

'I really got into being a parent and I'd play it the same in real life.'

'I played a parent who tried to understand.'

'Isn't it strange how kids blame their parents instead of themselves?'

Whether it is children playing at being grown-ups or courtiers advising their Queen, or teenagers working as doctors with the terminally ill or Kings placating the gods; whether it is the whole class expressing the thoughts of one mind, or one student playing many roles, it is the *active* engagement in the *imagined* situation which encourages the kinds of learning which drama promotes. These include weighing choices, facing consequences, considering implications, taking responsibility, asking questions, challenging authority, examining facts and finding significance in a world which is made by them and for them. It is the teacher, knowing what to do and why, who guides and holds them in that fictional world. For although drama is not often about finding solutions, the satisfaction that comes from being a part of the struggle helps students to view themselves not only as people *to whom* things happen but as people who can *make* things happen.

'If you were a teenager and all your friends were telling you to try drugs and you really didn't want to, what would you have to be to be able to say "No?" '
'You'd have to be brave.'
'You'd have to be your own person.'[1]

Reference
1 Teacher: Bev Haskins with Grade 4 students at Maplegrove Elementary School, St Catharine's, Ontario, 1983

Appendix 1

(Reference page 16)

Down the rabbit hole

In this game A is usually called 'the fox' and B 'the rabbit'. However, the teacher in Lesson 3 of Chapter 1 deliberately makes a point of referring to A and B as 'the hunter' and 'the hunted' because of her Dramatic Focus.

1 Participants scatter in pairs, facing each other with outstretched arms, fingers touching.
2 Teacher selects one pair: A is the hunter, B is the hunted.
3 At a signal from the teacher, A chases B who seeks refuge in a 'hole' created by another pair.
4 B then joins hands with the partner he faces. The one upon whom he has turned his back becomes 'the hunted' and is now chased by A.
5 Should A (the hunter) catch B (the hunted), the roles are reversed and 'the hunted' becomes 'the hunter' and so on.

Note: Once the rules are understood, the game is fast-moving, generally noisy and yet demands considerable physical control from all the participants.

Appendix 2a

(Reference for page 197)

Project Assessment Form

Student's name: Mary Queenston

Project: Anthology

In order to complete the project, you are asked to fill out this form and attach it to the other materials you are to hand in. You are to think about each person's contribution, including your own, and put in the square a number between 1 and 6 (1 being the low number and 6 the high number). This will help us when we talk together at the end of the term.

Student name:	Sally	Wade	Grant	Mary	Roz	Group average
works with commitment, interest and effort	5	4	5	5	5	24/30
works independently	5	2	3	5	2	17/30
works cooperatively in groups	2	5	6	4	5	22/30
explores ideas	6	5	6	4	5	26/30
expresses ideas	3	2	6	2	2	15/30
makes decisions	4	2	4	2	2	14/30
perseveres	5	6	6	5	6	28/30
completes assignments	3	5	6	3	6	23/30
demonstrates leadership	6	3	5	1	2	17/30
evaluates fairly and constructively	3	3	6	3	2	17/30
Individual mark (out of 60)	42	37	53	34	37	203

Group mark: 68

General comments: This was a really good group to work with and I think the audience really enjoyed what we did, but a lot of it was thanks to Grant! but I felt kind of useless sometimes.

(Teacher's comment to Mary at the interview: 'I think you undermarked yourself, Mary. The rest of the group rated your contributions much more highly.')

Appendix 2b

(Reference for page 197)

Individual Student Project Assessment Form (example)

In groups we all play a number of roles. The list below identifies some of these roles. Which roles did you play and when? Which roles were new to you and how comfortable did you feel using them? Place a percentage besides those roles which you took. These should add up to 100% in each of the projects. This sheet will be useful for us when we talk at the end of term.

Name: William Reece	*Project 1* Picture Book (Depictions):	*Project 2* Anthology	*Project 3* Masks
Leader by choice:			
Leader by election:			50% A good group to work with.
Leader by default:			
Positive follower:		40% I was with a group I didn't know.	30% Interesting project!
Ideas person:		40% Some of my ideas were used.	
Negative follower:	50% Nobody would listen.		
Iconoclast:			10% We were getting smug!!
Absentee:	50% I was ill with flu for most of it.		
Nurturer:			10% I really tried this time!
Doer:		20% We all helped.	
Your comments:	I was not in on the planning and had no interest.	A good project, we all got on well.	Discovered that I am a good leader with a hard-working group.
Teacher's comments:	Not a good experience for Bill.	Still tries to press the 'task' at the expense of group health.	Really learning to maintain group, does better when leader!

Appendix 3

(Reference for page 202)

The Big Rig Safety Co.
56 Cross Street
Cansville, Ontario
L30 5G7

15/4/85

Promotion Department
General Motors Trucking Division
St Catharines, Ontario

Dear Sirs

We thank you for your offer to buy the designs of Safety Big Rigs from our company. We have decided to continue to produce them at our own plant, under our direct supervision.

Thank you for your interest.

Yours faithfully

George Sparrow
Head Designer

Appendix 4

(Reference page 205)

Excerpt from a student Journal

Monday, January 14, 1986
1   Groups of 3: Lance, Allison and me.
    Make a very short, sharp scene which illustrates Jane's
    concept of time.
    Our scene
    Jane graduates from Law School. Upon receiving congratu-
    lations (and the gift of an hour-glass) from Patty, she says
    that she doesn't really want to be a lawyer, 'Maybe I'll be a
    doctor or a secretary, I just don't know.'
    Other scenes
    Having nothing to do with her time as a child.
    Being late and inappropriately dressed for a basketball
    practice.
    Having co-workers cover up for her absence by doing her
    work.
    Not wanting to play with the other kids.
    Setting up her timetable so that she can have Mondays and
    Thursdays off.

What we learned from these scenes:
only child
lonely, passive, frustrated child
indecisive
irresponsible
likeable person

2   Round circle, in chairs (although we usually sit on the floor,
    I liked sitting on chairs today)

Scene 1
Patty buying the hour-glass
Storekeeper: Sandra   Patty: me
Patty unsure of what to buy, wanting something related to time.
Storekeeper very helpful, suggests hour-glass which Patty likes.
This sort of improvisation is fun, your mind just seems to flow,
somehow the reactions seem automatic. Afterwards you wonder
what made you come up with that phrase or question or twist.

Scene 2
Patty buying the hour-glass
Storekeeper: Mike   Patty: Janice
Patty unsure of what to buy, storekeeper suggests a watch.
Patty sees hour-glass and decides on that.
Similar to Scene 1, except that Patty finds the hour-glass herself
in this one.

Scene 3
Patty buying the hour-glass
Storekeeper: Mark   Patty: Heidi
Patty asks for an hour-glass.
Storekeeper says 'no', then finds one, price $34.95.
Patty says 'no problem'.
Different scene because of Patty's sureness.
In all three scenes the gift was more important than the price.

Scene 4
Patty talking to friends about the gift
Patty: Julie   Friends: (−) Grant, (+) Colleen
Patty loves it.
Grant thinks it may be tacky and inappropriate.
Colleen loves it.
Patty needs to be careful to give the gift in the right way so that
Jane won't think it tacky.

Scene 5
Jane ill at work
Jane: Michelle   Office workers: Elaine and Leslie   Boss:
Martyn
Jane says her hands are sore, apologises that others had to do
her work and that she was late, says she's OK, just tired, from
the weekend camping trip.
Co-worker says it's been going on for six weeks.
Co-worker suggests a visit to the doctor.

Boss gives her opportunity to take time off.
They convince her to go home.

Scene 6
Jane's thoughts during her walk home
Inside Jane's head, her thoughts during walk home: everyone.
Scared, upset (why me?)
Embarrassed at being sent home from work
Keeps telling herself that it's all paranoia, there's nothing wrong
that sleep won't cure
Wanting to phone Patty
Tired, cold, sore hands
Amazing how there wasn't much overlap of people talking,
everyone along the same track.
I felt very sorry for Jane.

Scene 7
Doctor telling Jane the test results
Jane: Lance   Doctor: Grant
Jane cries throughout
Doctor very serious – bone cancer – no false hopes but the possi-
bility of a remission. Crisis number for help in dealing with it, 'I
wish I could do more.'
Probably six months to live

For Scenes 6 and 7, we turned our backs to the centre so we
couldn't see each other.

An interesting morning. It's easy to become very involved in the
story.

1   As Jane: (writing in role)
    'Oh, my God, how can this be happening to me? This is a
    dream, a bad dream, I'll wake up and it will be all right.
    No, it's not a dream. I'm dying. Why me? I can't tell anyone,
    they'll just feel sorry for me. There's so much I want to do.
    Oh, someone help me!'

2   As myself:
    Very sad, realistic, felt almost ready to cry with 'Jane'.

Bibliography

Abrams, M. H. (General Editor), *The Norton Anthology of English Literature*, W. W. Norton and Company, New York, 1975

Ambrus, V. G., *The Three Poor Tailors*, Harcourt Brace Inc., New York, 1965

Appel, Libby, *Mask Characterization: An Acting Process*, Southern Illinois University Press, 1982

Avital, Samuel, *Mime Work Book*, Lotus Light Publications, Wisconsin, 1982

Barton, Robert *et al.*, *Nobody in the Cast*, Longmans Canada, Don Mills Ontario, 1969

Barton, Robert, *Tell Me Another*, Pembroke, Markham, Ontario, 1986

British Broadcasting Company, *Three Looms Waiting*, Omnibus Documentary Film, 1971

Bennett, Stuart, *Drama: The Practice of Freedom*, National Association for the Teaching of Drama, London, 1984

Berry, Cicely, *Your Voice and How to Use it Successfully*, Harrap and Co., London, 1975

Bloom, Benjamin S. and Krathwohl David R., *Taxonomy of Educational Objectives, The Classification of Educational Goals*, D. McKay Co., New York, 1965

Bolton, Gavin M., *Drama as Education*, Longman, Harlow, England, 1984

Bolton, Gavin M., *Towards a Theory of Drama in Education*, Longman, London, 1979

Bond, Edward, *On Problems*

Boorman, Joyce, *Creative Dance in Grades Four to Six*, Longman Canada, Don Mills, Ontario, 1971

Boorman, Joyce, *Creative Dance in the First Three Grades*, Longman Canada, Don Mills, Ontario, 1969

Boorman, Joyce, *Dance and Language Experience with Children*, Longman Canada, Don Mills, Ontario, 1973

Booth, David, Barton, Robert and Buckles, Agnes, *Colours: A Language Arts Programme*, Longman Canada, Don Mills, Ontario, 1974

Booth, David, *Games for Everyone*, Pembroke, Markham, Ontario, 1986

Broadfoot, Barry, *Six War Years*, Doubleday Canada, Toronto, Ontario, 1974

Broadfoot, Barry, *Ten Lost Years*, Doubleday Canada, Toronto, Ontario, 1973

Burke, M. R. and Saxton, J. M., 'A piece of grit', *London Drama*, vol. 6, no. 10, 1984

Burke, M. R. and Saxton, J. M., 'Evaluation in drama', *Association of British Columbia Educator's Journal*, vol. 6, no. 1, 1984

Byron, Ken and Griffin, Dierdre, 'Still image', *Association of British Columbia Drama Educators*, vol. 5, no. 2, December 1983

Callow, Simon, *Being an Actor* (part two), Methuen, London, 1984

Chilver, Peter and Gould, Gerard, *Learning and Language in the Classroom*, Pergamon Press, Great Britain, 1982

Coger, Leslie and White, Melvin, *Reader's Theatre Handbook* (revised), Scott Foresman and Company, Glenview, Illinois, 1973

Cook, Pat, 'Evaluating drama', *2 D*, vol. 2, no. 1, Leicester, England, Summer 1982

Crampton, Esme, *Good Words Well Spoken*, Norman Press, Toronto, 1980

Crichton, E., *The Great Train Robbery*, Knopf, New York City, 1975

Currell, David, *Learning With Puppets*, Ward Lock Educational, London, 1980

Davies, Geoff. C., *Practical Primary Drama*, Heinemann Educational Books, London, 1983

Davies, H., 'Learning goals and personal autonomy', *Drama Broadsheet*, vol. 1, no. 1, Autumn, 1983

Davies, H., 'An operational approach to evaluation', in Day, Christopher and Norman (eds), *Issues in Educational Drama*, Palmer Press, London, 1983

Davis, David, 'Gavin Bolton Interviewed by David Davis', *L.D.*, vol. 4, no. 2, Spring 1985

Davis, D. and Lawrence, C. (eds), *Selected Writings on Drama in Education*, Longmans, London, 1986

DuMaurier, Daphne, *Rebecca*, Victor Gollancz Ltd, London, 1938

Evans, D. R., Hearn M. T., Uhlemann M., and Ivery A. E., *Essential Interviewing*, Brooks/Cole, Monterey, California, 1979

Ferguson, Marilyn, *The Aquarian Conspiracy*, Houghton Mifflin Co., 1980

Fines, John and Verrier, Raymond, *The Drama of History: An Experience in Co-operative Teaching*, New University Education, London, 1974

Fluegelman, Andrew (ed.), *More New Games*, Doubleday, New York, 1981

Fluegelman, Andrew (ed.), *The New Games Book*, Dolphin Books, Garden City, New York, 1976

Fowler, H. W. and Fowler F. G., *A Concise Oxford Dictionary of Current English*, 6th ed., 1977

Goffman, Erving, *1961 Encounters: Two Studies in the Sociology of Interaction*, Bobs Merrill, Indianapolis, 1962

Hamblin, K., *Mime: A Playback of Silent Phantasy*, Doubleday, New York, 1978

Heathcote, D. and Herbert, P., 'A drama of learning: Mantle of the Expert', *Theory into Practice*, vol. 24, no. 3, Summer 1985

Heathcote, D., *Specialization in Dramatic Arts*, Summer Course, Faculty of Education, University of Toronto, Ontario, 1973

Johnstone, Keith, *Impro*, Methuen, London, 1981

Johnson, D. W. and Johnson, F. P., *Joining Together: Group Therapy and Group Skills*, Prentice Hall Inc., New Jersey

Johnson, Liz and O'Neill, Cecily (eds), *Dorothy Heathcote: Collected Writings on Education and Drama*, Hutchinson, London, 1984

Julian, Nancy R., *Miss Picket's Secret, Brown is the Back of a Toad*, Longman's Canada, 1974

King, Nancy, *Giving Form to Feeling*, Drama Book Specialists, New York, 1975

Koestler, Arthur, *Beyond Reductionism: New Perspectives in the Life Sciences*, Hutchinson, 1969

Koppell, Tina, 'What is meant by drama in depth', *FINE* (Journal of the Fine Arts Council of the Alberta Teacher's Association), Alberta, Summer 1983

Krathwohl, D. (ed.), *Developing a Scale to Measure Affective Sensitivity*, Bureau of Educational Research Services, Michigan State University, East Lansing M.I., 1965

Leese, Sue and Palmer, Moira, *Dance in the Schools*, Heinemann Educational Books, 1980

Linnell, Rosemary, *Approaching Classroom Drama*, Edward Arnold, London, 1982

Lundy, Charles and Booth, David, *Improvisation*, Academic Press Canada, Don Mills, Ontario, 1985

Lundy, Charles and Booth, David, *Interpretation: Working With Scripts*, Academic Press Canada, Don Mills, Ontario, 1983

Lynch, Fraser, *Dance Play: Creative Movement for Very Young Children*, New American Library, New York, 1982

Martignone, Margaret E., The Illustrated Treasury of Children's Literature: 'Rumplestiltskin', by the Brothers Grimm, Grosset and Dunlap, New York, 1955

Matlock, Tim, 'Let's evaluate assessment', *Association of British Columbia Educators*, vol. 6, no. 1, 1984

McAra, Don, Drama Department Christchurch Teacher's College, New Zealand, Thesis (First Draught)

McDermott, Gerald, *Sunflight*, Scholastic Inc., Canada, 1984

Moffett, James and Wagner, Betty J., *A Student Centred Language Arts and Reading Curriculum: Grades K – 13*, 3rd ed., Haughton Mifflin, Boston, 1983

Moffett, James, *Teaching the Universe of Discourse*, Houghton Mifflin, Boston, 1982

Morgan, N. H. and, Saxton, J. M., 'Structures, strategies and techniques', *Canadian Child and Youth Drama Association Journal*, 1983

Morgan, John and Rinvolucri, Mario, *Once Upon a Time: Using Stories in the Language Classroom*, Cambridge University Press (U.S.A.), 1983

Nemiroff *et al.*, *Words on Work*, Globe/Modern Curriculum Press, Toronto, 1981

Nicholls, Bronwen, *Move! Plays*, Boston, 1975

Nixon, Jon (ed.), *Drama and the Whole Curriculum*, Hutchinson, London, 1982

O'Neill, Cecily *et al.*, *Drama Guidelines*, Heinemann Educational Books, London, 1976

O'Neill, Cecily and Lambert, Alan, *Drama Structures: A Practical Handbook for Teachers*, Hutchinson, London, 1982

Ontario Ministry of Education, *Dramatic Arts: Intermediate and Senior Divisions*, 1981

Opie, Iona and Opie, Peter, *Children's Games in Street and Playground*, Oxford University Press, London, 1969

Orlick, Terry, *Co-operative Sports and Games Book*, Pantheon Books, New York, 1982

Rist, Ray, 'On the application of ethnographic inquiry to education: procedures and possibilities', *Journal of Research in Science Teaching*, vol. 19, no. 6, 1982

Rolfe, Bari, *Behind the Mask*, Persona Books, California, 1977

Rothenberg, Jerome (ed.), *Technicians of the Sacred*, Doubleday Anchor Book, 1969

Schafer, R. M., *Ear Cleaning: Notes for an Experimental Music Course*, B.M.I. Canada, Don Mills, Ontario, 1967

Schafer, R. M., *When Words Sing*, Berandol Music, Scarborough, Ontario, 1970

Shurtleff, Michael, *Audition*, Walker and Co., New York, 1978

St. Denis, Michel, *Training for the Theatre*, Theatre Arts Books, New York, 1982

Stewig, John, *Spontaneous Drama: A Language Art*, Charles E. Harrell Publishing Co., Columbus, Ohio, 1973

Stolyenberg, Mark, *Exploring Mime*, Sterling Publishing Co., New York, 1983

Styan, J. L., *The Drama Experience*, Cambridge University Press, 1965

Taba, Hilda, *Teacher's Handbook for Elementary School Studies*, Addison-Wesley Publishing Co., Don Mills, Ontario, 1967

Tarlington, Carole and Verriour, Patrick, *Offstage: Elementary Education through Drama*, Oxford University Press, Toronto, 1983

Taylor, J. L. and Walford, R., *Simulation in the Classroom*, Penguin Papers in Education, Harmondsworth, 1972

Thomas, Dylan, *A Child's Christmas in Wales*, New Directions, Norfolk, Connecticut, 1954

Wagner, Betty-Jane, *Dorothy Heathcote: Drama as a Learning Medium*, National Education Association, Washington D. C., 1976

Way, Brian, *Development Through Drama*, Longmans, London, 1967

Index